Avoiding Age Discrimination

A Practical Guide to Managing a Changing Workforce

Avoiding Age Discrimination

A Practical Guide to Managing a Changing Workforce

an EEF guide

Published in 2006 by
EEF
Broadway House
Tothill Street
London SW1H 9NQ
www.eef.org.uk

In association with Profile Books Ltd
www.profilebooks.com

10 9 8 7 6 5 4 3 2 1

Text design by Sue Lamble
Typeset in FS Albert by MacGuru Ltd
info@macguru.org.uk

Printed and bound in Great Britain by Bell & Bain Ltd, Glasgow

A CIP catalogue record for this book is available from the British Library.

ISBN-10: 1 903461 79 0
ISBN-13: 978 1 903461 79 2

Disclaimer

This publication is based on our understanding of the law as at April 2006. It is intended to provide general guidance only. The publication is not intended to replace the need to obtain proper advice in relation to any matter discussed. EEF is not responsible for any acts or omissions arising from the use of this publication. More detailed advice on particular issues is available through your EEF Association.

Contents

1

Introduction

The changing labour market

Now is the time for employers to adopt a new attitude to age. There are two reasons for this. First, there are significant changes taking place in the UK labour market. The number of those in the workforce over the age of 50 is increasing, while the number of younger workers is declining. Half of all adults will be 50 or more by the year 2024. In 2010, 40 per cent of the workforce will be 45 or older. At the same time, employers seeking skilled workers are experiencing serious recruitment problems.

To overcome these difficulties, you, as an employer, will increasingly need to ensure you look at the widest possible pool of talent, both young and old, and do not limit your search by irrelevant criteria. You will need to focus on retaining skilled and knowledgeable workers rather than losing them just because they are older. At the other end of the scale, you will need to focus on the talents and abilities of younger workers rather than excluding them from consideration for recruitment and promotion just because they are young.

To stay ahead of the competition as the labour market changes, your business will need to react early. There is, however, another vital reason why you need to address the question of ageism in the workplace right now.

New laws

As of 1 October 2006, British and Northern Irish law prohibits age discrimination and gives a remedy in the employment tribunals to victims, who potentially could be awarded unlimited compensation.

The Employment Equality (Age) Regulations 2006 ('the Regulations'), the British legislation on age discrimination, constitute the last of the provisions implementing into British law the EU Employment Directive (2000/78), which has already led to regulations outlawing discrimination on the grounds of religion and belief or sexual orientation in the area of employment. We deal with the British regulations in this book, but those that apply to Northern Ireland are identical in all material aspects.

The provisions of the Regulations are described in detail in Appendix 1. We outline their important aspects here. The Regulations apply to young people, old people and those in between. They:

- prohibit unjustified age discrimination in employment and vocational training;
- require employers who set their retirement age below the age of 65 to justify or change it;
- introduce a duty on employers to consider an employee's request to continue working beyond retirement age;
- require employers to inform employees in writing, at least six months in advance, of the date when they intend employees to retire;
- remove the upper age limit for unfair dismissal and redundancy rights; and
- include provisions relating to service-related benefits and occupational pensions.

The scheme of the legislation

The Regulations follow the pattern of the earlier discrimination laws:

- They apply to people at work (employees, workers, contract workers) and to job applicants.
- They make direct discrimination unlawful – i.e. treating people less favourably because of their age, or their apparent age.

- They make indirect discrimination unlawful – i.e. treating everyone the same if that unjustifiably creates a disadvantage for people in a particular age group. (An example might be requiring all candidates for a job to have grey hair. This would exclude more younger people than older people from consideration for the post.)
- They outlaw harassment of people at work (whether by management or co-workers) on the grounds of age.
- They prohibit victimisation of someone for relying on the age legislation.

There are some important differences between the age legislation and other regulations dealing with unlawful discrimination.

Justifying discrimination

First, the employer has the defence of 'justification', whether the claim against it is for direct or indirect discrimination. This means that you, as the employer, will escape liability if you can show the tribunal that what you did was 'a proportionate means of achieving a legitimate aim' (these are the words used in the legislation).

So, not only can you potentially justify making use of an apparently non-discriminatory, across-the-board practice even though it disadvantages a particular age group; you may also be able to justify treating someone less favourably because of their age (or apparent age), *if* you have the evidence to do so.

We look at the issue of justifying discriminatory practices and actions in more detail in Chapter 3. The age discrimination legislation also provides a special form of justification in relation to the award of benefits based on length of service.

Exemptions

The second major difference between the age legislation and previous discrimination law is that the government has taken advantage of provisions in the Directive which permit it to carve out a range of employment benefits and practices which might otherwise be regarded as discriminatory.

So, for example, a refusal to recruit people over the age of 65, many aspects of pension provision and awarding benefits to employees on the basis of their having up to five years' service cannot be challenged under the Regulations. We consider the exemptions in more detail in the following chapters.

Proving and disproving discrimination

In a tribunal claim for age discrimination, it is for the claimant to show facts which, if they went unchallenged, would be sufficient for an employment tribunal to conclude there had been discrimination. If they do so, it is then up to the employer to prove that what the claimant says is simply untrue, or that its treatment of the claimant was in no sense whatsoever related to the claimant's age, or that it was justified. If the employer cannot satisfy the tribunal on one of these grounds, the tribunal *must* find for the claimant.

The facts that the claimant needs to prove to put this burden of disproving discrimination on you, as the employer, are quite straightforward.

In a claim of direct discrimination, the claimant needs to prove that there was a difference in treatment and in age between him or herself and an actual or hypothetical person whose circumstances are essentially the same. An example of this might be where an older employee is selected for redundancy rather than a younger employee.

In a claim of indirect discrimination, the claimant needs to prove that the claimant and people in the same age group suffer (or would suffer) a disadvantage by reason of your practices, and this disadvantage is not (or would not) be suffered by other people. An example could be the selection of a young person for redundancy on the basis of their relatively short service if, in that selection pool, the older employees have longer service than the younger employees.

In each of these redundancy examples, the claimant has shown facts which, if they went unchallenged, would be sufficient to enable the tribunal to conclude there had been discrimination. It is now for you, as the employer, to prove that you did not discriminate unlawfully.

Continuing with the redundancy examples, you would have to prove that your selection procedures were in no way related to age, (so that, for example, service was not a factor in selection), or that your selection procedures were justified in that they were a proportionate means of achieving a legitimate aim (Chapter 3 deals with justification in detail). This would require clear and cogent evidence demonstrating that age played no part in your decision or, if it did, that your practice was justified. If the tribunal is left in doubt, it will find against you. Redundancy is examined in detail in Chapter 9.

Comparators

It is important to remember that someone who claims that they have been subjected to age discrimination must always prove either that they have been (or would have been) treated less favourably than a comparable person of a different age, or that they have been disadvantaged by a provision, criterion or practice (PCP) used by the employer, while comparable individuals of a different age group have not been (or would not be) disadvantaged.

In principle, when comparing the impact of a PCP on different age groups, it is the scope of the PCP that determines the categories of people who can be included in the comparison. So, if your recruitment practices are at issue, the appropriate groups to compare may be those in the job market who are otherwise qualified for appointment or even those in the working age population generally. If the PCP merely affects your own workforce, as in the case of redundancy selection criteria, the appropriate population will be your workforce in the areas subject to the redundancy exercise.

Other guidance on the Regulations

Unlike other areas of discrimination, there is no statutory code of practice on avoiding age discrimination in employment. ACAS has issued guidance on the Regulations ('Age and the Workplace: Putting the Employment Equality (Age) Regulations 2006 into Practice') which contains useful good practice recommendations, although the guidance does not have the force of law. This is available on the ACAS website, www.acas.org.uk.

Separate guidance has also been issued by the government in respect of the Regulations provisions on pensions. Chapter 14 gives further detail.

2

Being prepared

The age discrimination legislation has a vast potential impact because it covers all individuals of all ages who work for you or who apply to you for jobs. Because of this, it may seem difficult to know where to start in ensuring that your practices comply with the legislation. We suggest that, as a starting point, you assess the risk areas in your practices and also monitor the age profile of your workforce, so that you can identify how vulnerable you may be to successful age discrimination claims and take appropriate action.

Risk assessment and monitoring

To assess the potential impact on your business of the age legislation, we recommend you should first set out the areas of your business where the legislation could have an impact. The topics covered in this Guide will assist in this.

You should then review your practices and policies in these areas, using the information contained in this Guide. If there are any which make explicit reference to age or length of service, you should first check whether there is an exemption under the Regulations permitting your current practice or policy to continue. If not, you need to consider whether you have evidence to show that it is a proportionate means of achieving a legitimate aim (see Chapter 3). If not, you will need to change the relevant policy or practice. Chapter 11 gives further advice on the steps you could take.

The next stage of the review is to look at the age profile of those affected by your policies and practices. Many employers are already aware of the ages of their employees and of the average age of their workforce. However, as well as looking at the overall make-up of your workforce, you will gain a better understanding of the potential impact of the age legislation if you look, in particular, at the ages of:

- job applicants and compare them with those who are ultimately recruited;
- those who are offered training or who are promoted and those who are not;
- those who leave the employment of the company, whether by reason of redundancy or retirement.

The aim is to get an impression of what impact your policies and practices have had on particular age groups. If there is a marked disparity between one age group and others in terms of who benefits or suffers from a policy or practice, you will need to consider whether the statistics reveal a real problem or are the result simply of the sample size being too small to be meaningful.

If the statistics are significant, you will need to consider whether the policy or practice is expressly permitted by the Regulations or, if not, is justified. If there is no exemption and the policy or practice is likely to prove difficult to justify, you will again need to change it for the future.

Note that you will not be liable for discrimination where disparities between age groups result from events or practices or policies which had their effect exclusively prior to 1 October 2006.

Areas for risk assessment

What areas do you have to think about in seeking to address the risk of future age discrimination complaints?

Retirement

Retirement is a key issue. By way of exception from the general rule against age discrimination, the Regulations permit employers to enforce retirement at age 65 or, if their normal retirement age is higher, at that age. It is age discrimination to make an employee retire at a lower age, unless you can justify requiring retirement at that lower age (which will be very difficult). Forcing an employee to retire may also amount to an unfair dismissal. Of course, if an employee wants to retire, no legal issue arises.

You may decide (for example, because you wish to retain skills in the business) that you no longer wish to enforce retirement, leaving it to employees to decide when to retire and dealing with employees who are reluctant to retire through performance management.

You may also decide that you wish to encourage older employees to work on to, or beyond, normal retirement age by offering flexible working options.

If you want to take advantage of your ability under the Regulations to insist on employees retiring at 65 or at a higher age, you must give at least six months' notification to the employee of the intended date of retirement and of the employee's right under the Regulations to request not to retire. If an employee makes such a request, you must consider it. You therefore need to have a procedure for notifying employees of retirement and for considering requests not to retire and these must comply with the legal requirements. You also need to make a decision on the strategy to adopt for dealing with requests not to retire. We provide guidance on all these issues in Chapters 4–8.

Redundancy

Redundancy is an area where, potentially, age legislation could have a significant impact. The Regulations do exempt the statutory redundancy payments scheme from legal challenge and grant protection for employer 'top-up' schemes that mirror the statutory scheme. But it is not simply in respect of termination payments that considerations of age and service may come into play in the process of making redundancies.

Length of service may be the sole or one of a number of criteria used for selecting those to be made redundant from a pool of employees; this may indirectly discriminate against younger employees. Volunteers may be sought for early retirement, but this offer is likely to be open only to those aged 55 and over. Consciously or unconsciously, age itself, or such things as the cost of redundancy payments, closeness to retirement or having family responsibilities (all of which are age-related), may influence the choices managers make about who should be selected.

We consider the impact of age discrimination legislation on all of these issues, whether the use of age and/or service can be justified in these contexts and what steps an employer should take to try to avoid any discrimination, in Chapter 10.

Pay and benefits

The situation regarding pay and benefits under the age legislation is somewhat complex. The basic proposition is that where an award of pay or a particular benefit is dependent on the employee attaining a particular age or length of service, the employer would need to be able to justify that requirement by showing that it was a proportionate means of achieving a legitimate aim, otherwise the employer would be vulnerable to a claim for age discrimination. However, the legislation protects you from such claims where the pay or benefit was awarded under statutory authority, as with statutory redundancy payments or payments in compliance with the National Minimum Wage legislation. It also protects you if you apply more generous benefits which correspond to a statutory scheme.

In addition, service-related benefits based on five years' service or less are permitted. Where benefits are awarded on the basis of longer periods of service, a special test of justification applies. Under this, if it reasonably appears to the employer that it fulfils a business need (such as encouraging loyalty or rewarding experience) to make the award of a benefit dependent on having a particular period of service, the practice will be regarded as justified.

We examine the range of age- or service-related benefits that an employer might offer, and consider the potential impact of the legislation upon them in Chapter 10. Where changes might be required in the provision of benefits because their lawfulness is in doubt, we advise on your options.

Recruitment

The area of recruitment is particularly one where ageism is likely to manifest itself. Employers or managers may deliberately or unconsciously target or exclude particular age groups when recruiting, either generally or for a particular post. This may be because they have in mind that particular posts are suited only to older or younger workers, or it may be to try to ensure the new appointee 'fits in' with the existing team. If you do disregard candidates outside a particular age range and are challenged by a rejected candidate, your only defence – assuming the rejected candidate is appropriately qualified – will be that you had a legitimate, non-discriminatory, purpose in mind in limiting your recruitment. You will need to persuade the tribunal that targeting or excluding particular age groups was a proportionate means of achieving that legitimate aim.

It seems to us unlikely that tribunals will regard achieving a 'balanced' workforce in terms of age as a legitimate recruitment aim. However, recruiting to try to ensure adequate succession planning (which, in practice, may amount to the same thing) may be regarded as a legitimate aim. You would then need to show that your business does indeed plan for succession, that the specific recruitment decision fits with the plan and that the plan is a proportionate response to the aim, taking into account, for example, the need to increase the diversity of the talent pool.

We look in more detail at the changes that may be needed to recruitment practices, in terms of advertising, application forms, interview panels and so on, in Chapter 12.

Performance management, training and promotion

There are other practices that you will have to consider in the light of age discrimination legislation. For example, what is your practice in relation to providing training opportunities for older workers? Is a different attitude taken by managers to performance appraisal of older rather than younger workers? Are younger, or older, workers excluded from consideration for promotion? We examine the areas where employment practice can fall foul of the age legislation in Chapter 13 and suggest approaches employers could adopt to avoid that result.

Harassment

The Regulations add harassment on the ground of age, whether by managers or by co-workers, to the existing unlawful harassment provisions (outlawing, for example, racial harassment, sexual harassment, etc.). You, as the employer, will be liable for such 'ageist' harassment and an employment tribunal may order you to pay the affected employee compensation, including compensation for injury to feelings, unless you have taken all reasonably practical steps to prevent the harassment occurring.

At the least, this means (i) you *must* have a policy against such behaviour, (ii) which is communicated to all employees, and (iii) you *must* ensure that all employees are trained in the importance of avoiding harassment.

We give advice in relation to such policies and training in Chapter 15.

3

Justification

If your review of policies and practices has brought to light a policy, criterion, practice or examples of treatment of individuals (all of which in this chapter we shall call a 'practice') that has discriminatory effects, and if it is not expressly permitted to continue by the Regulations, you need to consider whether it is justified.

To be justified, a practice must be 'a proportionate means of achieving a legitimate aim'. A practice that has a discriminatory effect will still be lawful if it meets the justification test but you as the employer must have evidence to show that it does.

Legitimate aim

Your first step in considering whether you can justify a practice is to identify the aim of, or reason for, the practice and whether this aim is legitimate. To be legitimate, the aim must relate to a reasonable need of the business. A difficulty here is that, under EU law, an employer seeking to justify discrimination cannot rely *solely* on considerations of cost. So, if the reason you do something that has a discriminatory effect is because it is cheaper than acting in a non-discriminatory way, you are not likely to be able to justify your actions. We consider this further below.

Proportionate response

Whatever your aim, what you do to achieve it must be proportionate, which means that the practice in question must be appropriate and reasonably necessary to achieving the aim and, in effect, the benefit of the practice to your business must outweigh its discriminatory effect.

There are three key elements to establishing that your practice is proportionate:

- You must be able to demonstrate that the practice does actually achieve, or will assist in achieving, its aim (i.e. that it is appropriate).
- You must establish that the particular practice is reasonably necessary: if your aim can be achieved by another practice that is not discriminatory or is less discriminatory, then you are unlikely to be able to establish this.
- You need to weigh up, as objectively as possible, the discriminatory effect of the practice against the importance of its aim. The greater the discriminatory effect of the practice, the more compelling must be its benefits.

Cost and justification

As we stated above, the courts have decided that cost alone cannot be a sufficient justification.

However, you can put the aim of cost-saving into the balance together with other justifications, if there are any. For example, if you select young, short-service employees for redundancy because it is cheaper than selecting older, longer-serving, employees, a tribunal will almost certainly find that to be unjustified and therefore unlawful discrimination. But if you were able to show evidence that, for example, in a particular redundancy exercise, it was vital to the continued viability of the business that the maximum cash was retained within the business, your aim of reducing the cost of the redundancy exercise will most probably be regarded as legitimate.

Framework for considering justification

We suggest adopting the following framework for considering justification, which is based on ACAS Guidance and EU case law. You can apply this framework whenever the issue of justifying potentially discriminatory treatment of a person, or the potentially discriminatory effects of a particular policy, criterion or practice (PCP) arises.

Legitimate aim

- Ask yourself 'Why do we want to do this, what is our aim?'
- Ask yourself whether your business reasonably needs to achieve that objective and, if so, why.

Proportionate means

- Ask yourself whether the practice achieves or goes towards achieving your objective – do you have evidence that shows this?
- Is there a less or non-discriminatory way of achieving the same result?
- If not, weigh up, as objectively as you can, the relative seriousness of the discriminatory effects of the policy or practice (for those disadvantaged) against the importance to the business of pursuing its aim – does the former outweigh the latter?

Credibility

- Ensure you have evidence to support your conclusions. Mere assertions are not enough.
- Seek a second opinion on these questions from a senior colleague.
- Ensure each step of this process is noted down.

Example of applying the framework

As an illustration of how to assess the risk of a claim and apply the justification test, suppose your company has a practice of not recruiting anyone over the age of 60. First, you consider whether there is an exemption under the

Regulations permitting the practice to continue. In this case, the legislation provides an exception that generally permits the practice of not recruiting those aged 64 and a half or over to continue (see Chapter 12). Your practice of not recruiting those in their early sixties is, however, vulnerable to challenge should anyone of that age apply and be rejected.

The evidence may show, however, that hardly anyone in that age group has, in fact, ever applied for a job with your company. That might suggest that this particular policy is a low priority to be addressed in terms of putting your house in order.

However, before coming to that conclusion, you should consider whether, in fact, there is something in your recruitment advertising that directly or indirectly discourages applications from older people. As the demography changes, issues of pensioner poverty come more to the fore and campaigns to encourage a longer working life take hold, more older people will be in the job market. Your practices may become increasingly vulnerable to challenge.

In order to justify your policy in the event of challenge, you need to ask first what the company's reason for this policy is: what is your aim? If there is no reason other than ageism, clearly the policy cannot be justified. A number of possible legitimate reasons suggest themselves for such a policy. One possibility is health and safety. This is most unlikely to justify a blanket refusal to recruit people over 60 but there may be one or two specific jobs where the evidence supports a recruitment cut-off age. However, you must have clear evidence, whether general or relating to the company's own experience, to support this. An assumption based on stereotypes will not do.

Two other factors mentioned in the Employment Directive (Article 6) may be relevant: the need for a reasonable period of employment before retirement and the training requirements of the post in question. The age legislation currently permits retirement to be enforced at 65. You could argue that, in order to make the cost and time of recruitment worthwhile, to enable new recruits to reach their full potential in the role and to maintain a stable workforce, you need to employ people for a reasonable period before their retirement at 65. Depending on staff turnover, the costs of recruitment and the 'lead-in time' required for the role, this would be likely to justify a policy of not recruiting 64-year-olds.

If the policy extends to not recruiting people in their early sixties, the question would then arise as to whether that was a proportionate response to the legitimate aim of ensuring a reasonable period of employment before retirement. If, for example, the evidence was that your staff turnover was relatively high, so that, in general, employees tended not to stay beyond two or three years, such a policy is unlikely to be justified because you lack the evidence to show that the policy achieves the aim. In industries or particular jobs with low retention rates, the policy will be more difficult to justify.

If, instead, you had evidence that a lengthy period of training was necessary before you could gain full benefit from employees in particular roles, that would justify a refusal to recruit where little or no benefit would be gained from the training before retirement, but it would not justify a blanket policy across all posts in the business.

If you do not have the evidence to justify your practice of not recruiting those over 60, you will need to change it.

Justifying service-related benefits

The Regulations provide a special test of justification in relation to the award of benefits based on length of service. It is not uncommon for employers to provide additional or enhanced benefits for employees who have reached a particular length of service. This might involve, for example, increasing their entitlement to sick pay or to paid holiday, or presenting them with a long-service award.

Requiring a lengthy period of service before a particular benefit is granted could be argued to disadvantage younger employees. Although younger employees have the potential to gain the benefit in the future, this practice may none the less amount to indirect discrimination. This is because the same requirement (having a particular length of service before you can get the benefit) is applied to everyone but, at any one time, it is likely in many workforces that those who do not meet the requirement will include more young people than those who do.

The Regulations treat these benefits as being justified if it reasonably appears to the employer that using service as a criterion for awarding the benefit in the way it does fulfils a business need.

So, for example, if the employment tribunal considers that it was reasonable for you, the employer, to consider that awarding increased holidays to employees after, say, 10, 15 and 20 years encourages their loyalty, an employee without the relevant service will not be able successfully to challenge the practice.

One way in which this form of justification differs from the usual test of justification (proportionate means of achieving a legitimate aim) is that it does not matter that the needs of the business could be fulfilled in an alternative, less discriminatory, way. So long as it reasonably appears to the employer that his practice of attaching the award of particular benefits to achieving particular periods of service fulfils a business need, it will be justified.

4

Introduction to retirement

The age discrimination legislation is very significant for retirement and raises a wide range of important issues. An entire section of this Guide is devoted to retirement, and is divided into the following chapters: Retirement ages (Chapter 5); Procedural steps for retirement (Chapter 6); Employees working beyond retirement age (Chapter 7); and Retirement and unfair dismissal (Chapter 8).

When we refer to retirement in this Guide, we mean the termination of employment by reason of an employee reaching a certain age. This is not the same as retirement in the sense of the time when an employee starts to draw his or her pension. Retirement age is not necessarily the same as pensionable age, the latter being the age at which an employee is entitled to draw a pension. Chapter 14 deals with how pensions are affected by the age discrimination legislation.

The key messages of the following chapters for you as the employer are as follows:

- Compulsory retirement (i.e. imposing retirement against the employee's wishes) at age 65 or over is not unlawful age discrimination.
- Compulsory retirement at any age lower than 65 is unlawful unless the employer can meet the test of justification. This will be very difficult.
- You should consider now what approach to take to retirement ages, and adopt a strategy for retirement.

- The Regulations set out procedural steps that you must follow when you intend to retire an employee. These are based on the employee's right to request not to retire.
- You must give written notification to the employee, at least six months in advance, of the date when you intend the employee to retire and of their right to request not to retire.
- If an employee makes a valid request, you have a duty to consider it and you must follow a specific procedure.
- Compulsory retirement – namely, requiring employees to retire against their wishes – will almost certainly amount to a dismissal in law.
- Employees aged 65 or over, or at the normal retirement age or over, have the right not to be unfairly dismissed.
- The 'normal retirement age' is an important concept for the provisions on unfair dismissal, and you need to identify this in respect of your employees.
- You will not be liable for unfair dismissal if you only retire employees once they have reached age 65 or a higher normal retirement age and you have followed the required procedural steps.
- If you agree to an employee working beyond retirement age, it is unlawful to offer less favourable pay and benefits to that employee on grounds of age unless you can justify this.

5

Retirement ages

This chapter outlines the exemption in the Regulations concerning compulsory retirement at age 65 and above and the difficulty of justifying it at a lower age. It identifies the options open to employers in respect of retirement ages in light of the legislation, and encourages employers to think about what strategy they should apply to retirement.

Age discrimination and retirement ages

Dismissing an employee because he or she has reached a certain age is age discrimination. However, by virtue of an express provision in the Regulations, compulsory retirement at age 65 and over is not unlawful. This means that, if you enforce a retirement age of 65 or over, or if you require employees to retire (against their wishes) when they are 65 or over, you will not discriminate unlawfully on grounds of age.

The position is different for compulsory retirement at ages lower than 65. Enforcing retirement ages lower than 65, or requiring employees to retire (against their wishes) when they are under 65, is unlawful unless you can meet the test of justification. Justification is explained in Chapter 3.

As we shall see in this chapter, one of the vital steps that employers should take in response to the age discrimination legislation is to consider the current retirement age(s) of their employees and to make decisions on whether to retain those ages, change them or remove them altogether.

Retirement at age 65 and above

Dismissal by reason of retirement at age 65 and over is expressly excluded from the scope of the Regulations. Employers can therefore be certain that compulsorily retiring an employee because he or she has reached age 65 or over is not unlawful age discrimination. (There may, however, be a risk of unfair dismissal, although the risk is far greater when compulsory retirement takes place below age 65. See Chapter 8.) The government refers to retirement at age 65 as the 'national default retirement age'.

The default retirement age has been a controversial matter and the government will review it in 2011. It is quite possible that the review will result in the exemption being removed, so that retirement at any age could be potentially unlawful age discrimination. This is a factor to bear in mind when you are considering whether to retain a retirement age at the moment or to remove it altogether.

For the time being, the legal position is that if you dismiss employees by reason of retirement (i.e. if you compulsorily retire them) at age 65 or over, you will not be discriminating unlawfully on grounds of age.

The exemption applies only to dismissal by reason of retirement; it does *not* mean that those aged 65 or over can *never* have an age discrimination claim. Employees aged 65 or over can pursue age discrimination claims on other grounds, such as harassment or the application of discriminatory terms and conditions (but note the exception for recruitment, which is considered in Chapter 12). They can also pursue age discrimination claims in respect of dismissal for reasons other than retirement.

So, for example, if you select a 66-year-old employee for redundancy on grounds of his or her age, then you cannot benefit from the exemption and may face liability for unlawful discrimination. You may also face liability for unfair dismissal because the upper age limits for claiming unfair dismissal no longer apply (see Chapter 8).

Retirement below age 65

Compulsorily retiring an employee below age 65 constitutes unlawful age discrimination, unless you can meet the test of justification (see Chapter 3). To do so, you must be able to show that the retirement age you have set is a *proportionate means of achieving a legitimate aim.*

Our view is that unless there are specific and compelling reasons for a retirement age lower than 65, it is unlikely that you will be able to justify it.

If you currently apply a retirement age lower than 65 to your workforce, the first thing to do is to think long and hard about whether you can justify it. It is important you do this as soon as possible, if you have not already done so. An example of how the justification test applies to a retirement age is given at the end of this chapter.

Bear in mind that even if you believe that you can justify the lower retirement age, you are still open to challenge and a tribunal may not agree with you. There is always going to be a risk that an employee can successfully challenge a retirement age lower than 65 as unlawfully discriminatory on grounds of age. A successful challenge by an employee whom you retired below age 65 can also result in a finding of unfair dismissal (see Chapter 8). The problem is, you will not know the answer to this question until you are taken to tribunal. This is a risk that many employers are not prepared to take.

Options for retirement ages

Part of your response to the age discrimination legislation should be to consider what approach to take to retirement ages. The age discrimination legislation heralds a change in attitudes towards retirement. In the coming years an increasing number of employees may wish to work for longer and exercise their right to request not to retire (see Chapter 6). Looking ahead to 2011, the government review may result in the removal of the default retirement age. For these reasons, even if you currently have a retirement age of

65 or above, you should assess what strategy you wish to apply to employees who wish to work beyond that age.

We identify below some different options open to you and the key considerations that arise for each. The strategy you choose will depend on the needs of your business and the circumstances of your workforce. You may also need to apply different strategies to different parts of the workforce depending on the nature of the jobs involved.

Raise the retirement age to 65 or over

You should be considering raising any retirement age that is lower than 65 because of the difficulty of meeting the justification test. As we have explained above, if you raise the retirement age to 65, you will not face age discrimination claims and you will benefit from greater protection against unfair dismissal claims.

Increasing the retirement age, say from 63 to 65, simply gives employees the choice to work for a longer period, if they wish. This still leaves them with the option of resigning at an earlier age, including when they reach the original retirement age. The key point is that increasing the retirement age to 65 means that employees will no longer be required to retire at 63 and can work for longer if they wish.

Bear in mind that the age at which employees retire is not necessarily the same as the age when they are entitled to draw their pension. It is only where you are considering raising both the retirement age and the pensionable age that employees could suffer adverse consequences. Pensions are considered in detail in Chapter 14.

Raising the retirement age may encourage more employees to continue working, which could mean that you retain valuable experience, and could assist in staff shortages and difficulties in recruitment.

Remove the retirement age

An alternative option is to remove the retirement age altogether. As with an increase in the retirement age, this simply gives employees the option of working for longer if they wish.

Again, removing the retirement age may encourage employees to continue working beyond their original retirement age, and this may alleviate staff shortages. Another benefit of having no retirement age is that no further action will be required in the event that the law changes after the 2011 review.

A retirement age is a catalyst for older employees to leave their employment. Without a retirement age, older employees are still likely to resign when they decide it is time to retire. If, on the other hand, you wish an older employee to retire but he or she is unwilling, then under the Regulations you still have the option of retiring him or her compulsorily. (This would require you to follow the procedural steps for retirement, explained in Chapter 6.)

Bear in mind that raising or removing the retirement age may require you to manage performance more closely if retirement has been used in the past (perhaps wrongly) as a substitute for addressing poor performance. Performance management is considered in Chapter 13. See also Appendix 2 for issues relating to managing an age-diverse workforce.

Practical steps for changing the current retirement age

There are certain steps we recommend you to take to implement your decision to raise the retirement age or remove it altogether.

Consult. You should consult with your employees about your proposal, and ensure that you explain its implications to them. A key message to get across is that increasing or removing the current retirement age means that in future you are not going to *require* your employees to retire at that age. Where the employees have a contractual retirement age, this means that you are not going to rely on that contractual term. Make sure that you also explain the interaction between the employees' pension arrangements and what you are proposing for the retirement age. (If you are also considering changing the pension arrangements, you will need detailed advice from your pension advisers and your EEF Association.)

Communicate the new retirement age. You must ensure that your decision is clearly communicated to all affected employees. You should, for example, issue a written announcement to the employees confirming your decision – namely, that the age at which they will be required to retire has been increased (and state the new retirement age), or that it has been removed altogether.

Adopting a strategy for retirement

Considering your options about retirement ages requires you to think not only about your obligations under the age discrimination legislation but also more generally about the future needs of your business, how your workforce can best meet these needs, and the implications of allowing employees to work for longer.

Employment and succession planning will be factors in your assessment. Your business may have an increasing need to retain older workers because of skills shortages amongst younger employees. Alternatively, you may have identified a need to focus on the development of younger employees who have a significant length of potential employment ahead of them, rather than seeking to retain those who have reached retirement age.

You should also investigate the potential financial and operational impact of allowing employees to work for longer (whether by agreeing to a request not to retire, by raising the retirement age or by removing it altogether). For example, you should ascertain the effects of employing an increasing number of older workers on matters such as your employer's liability insurance and the cost of providing medical insurance, permanent health insurance (PHI) cover and death-in-service benefit. Any potentially negative effects should be weighed up against the potential benefits of retaining employees who have reached retirement age (for example in terms of keeping their key skills and enabling these skills to be passed on to other employees).

Chapter 7 looks at how the age discrimination legislation impacts on decisions to allow employees to work beyond their retirement age, and you should bear these issues in mind. See also Appendix 2 on managing an age-inclusive workforce.

As well as making these strategic decisions, you need to address the administrative aspects of handling retirements to ensure that you comply with your obligations under the legislation and follow the required procedural steps. Chapter 6 gives more detail on implementing a retirement policy.

6

Procedural steps for retirement

The Regulations require employers to follow certain procedural steps when they wish to retire an employee. These are based on the employee's right to request not to retire, which is a new right introduced by the legislation.

The consequences of an employer failing to comply with the procedural steps are very serious. Failure to comply may allow the employee to obtain an award of compensation by complaint to an employment tribunal. In cases where the employee was retired against his or her wishes, it may also result in the tribunal making an automatic finding that the retirement was an unfair dismissal.

This chapter explains the steps of the procedure that you as the employer are required to follow under the Regulations. It is important to remember that this aspect of the legislation applies to employees only, and not to the wider category of workers.

When do the procedural steps apply?

You must follow the procedural steps whenever you intend to retire an employee. This includes employees whom you intend to retire for a second time because you agreed to a previous request for them to continue working.

It may be tempting not to follow the procedural steps for an employee who appears to be happy to retire, on the basis that they are unlikely to lodge a claim against you. However, this raises some potentially serious problems. The procedural steps require you to take action well in advance of the retirement date, and at that time you will not be certain whether the employee will retire willingly or whether you will have to retire him or her compulsorily. Indeed, you may even face circumstances where the employee raises no objection at the time of the retirement, but subsequently claims that the retirement was brought about against his or her wishes.

If you subsequently face an unfair dismissal claim, your defence will be far stronger if you have followed the procedural steps.

We therefore recommend that you follow the procedural steps for every employee you intend should retire, regardless of whether or not you think that they will be happy with your decision.

As we explain in Chapter 8, if you retire an employee before age 65, or before his or her normal retirement age if there is one, you cannot successfully defend an unfair dismissal claim. This is because you cannot argue that retirement was the reason for the termination of employment. For this reason, you should not attempt to retire employees below age 65/their normal retirement age. You should also not embark on this procedure in respect of employees who will be below that age at the time you intend their employment to terminate. For further details, see the section on 'Unfair retirements' in Chapter 8.

The procedural steps

This section describes the steps you are required to take under the Regulations when you wish to retire an employee. The core elements are as follows:

- You must give written notification to the employee of the date on which you intend retirement to take place and of the employee's right to request not to retire.
- You should ensure that you give this notification at least six months in advance of the date on which you intend retirement to take place. We refer to this as 'standard notification'.

- If you receive a request, you must follow a specific procedure to consider it, which involves holding a meeting with the employee to discuss it, and if necessary holding an appeal meeting.

Standard notification

The Regulations require you to give the following information in writing to the employee at least six months before the intended retirement date:

- the date on which you intend the employee to retire; and
- the employee's right to request not to retire on that date.

You must do this no more than one year and no later than six months before that date.

A sample standard notification is given in Appendix 5. You *cannot* satisfy this step by giving the information at an earlier date or in another form, such as by inserting it in the employment contract at the start of the employment or in an employee handbook. There are compelling reasons to ensure that you give standard notification:

- If you fail to do so, then the employee is entitled to complain to an employment tribunal and obtain an award of up to eight weeks' pay. This remedy is considered in more detail in Chapter 16.
- The retirement will not fall within the circumstances of a 'safe retirement', which give you protection against liability for unfair dismissal (see Chapter 8).
- If you give standard notification, then the employee has only a limited time in which to make a request not to retire (see below), which will assist your planning. If you miss the window, then the employee can make a last-minute request which you will have to consider.

We recommend that you allocate to a person in your company, such as the Human Resources Manager, the responsibility of maintaining a diary of all retirement dates, with reminders set at nine months prior to those dates, so that you do not miss the window you have for giving standard notifications.

Remember, you should not be giving standard notification to employees if the intended retirement date would fall before they reach age 65 or the normal retirement age if there is one. See further Chapter 8.

Fall-back notification

If you miss the window for standard notification, you remain under a duty to give the same written information to the employee, namely the date on which you intend the employee to retire and the right to request. You must do so at the latest by the *fourteenth day before their employment terminates.*

Although there are serious consequences of missing the standard notification window (see above), fall-back notification does at least give you the potential to be able to defend a claim of unfair dismissal. This is considered further in Chapter 8. However, fall-back notification is a last resort and you should always aim to give standard notification.

The employee's right to request not to retire

The Regulations give all employees the right to request not to retire. This means that (as long as the employee makes a valid request) you have a duty to consider it by following a specific procedure.

A request is valid if made at one of the following two times:

- If you have given the standard notification, then the employee must make the request between six and three months before the intended date of retirement. If the request is made later, it is not valid and it does not trigger your duty to consider it.
- If you have missed the window for standard notification, then the employee can make a request at any time in the six months before the intended date of retirement. This means that you could receive a last-minute request and you would have the duty to consider it. You are not, however, required to consider a request made after employment has terminated.

To be valid, the employee's request must be made at the correct time. It could take the form of a letter, memorandum or e-mail and it must meet the following conditions:

- The request must be in writing and state that it is made under paragraph 5 of Schedule 6 of the Employment Equality (Age) Regulations 2006.
- The request must propose that the employment continues beyond the intended date of retirement either indefinitely, or for a stated period, or until a stated date.
- If you have failed to give either standard or fall-back notification at the time the employee makes the request, the request must identify the date on which the employee believes you intend their retirement to take place.

The request relates solely to not retiring, rather than changing the existing terms and conditions. However, in practice you are likely to receive requests to continue working beyond retirement but on different terms and conditions. As long as the request meets the conditions above, then it will be valid and you will have a duty to consider it, even if it goes further than a request simply to continue working on the same terms. The legal implications of applying different terms and conditions are considered in Chapter 7.

Procedure for considering a request

If you receive a valid request, you have the duty to consider it. To comply with this duty, you must follow the procedure set out below. Appendix 6 contains sample letters for use under this procedure.

It is vitally important to comply with all the aspects of the procedure, including the requirements for decision letters. Failure to comply will result automatically in an unfair dismissal.

Hold a meeting

On receipt of a request, you must hold a meeting with the employee within a reasonable time.

You may face a situation where the employee makes a request at the earliest possible time – six months before the intended date of retirement – and it is too early for you to decide on your response. If this is the case, you should write to the employee to explain the situation and state an approximate date in the future when you will hold a meeting. If you obtain the employee's agreement to this, it will be difficult for them to argue that the meeting was not held within a reasonable time. Alternatively you could try to persuade the employee to withdraw the request and represent it later, on the basis that if you have to make a decision now, you will almost certainly have to refuse the request.

The purpose of the meeting is to discuss the request. You should therefore ensure that the employee is given a proper opportunity to put forward the reasons why he or she does not wish to retire, to explain his or her proposal, and that these issues are discussed.

Give your decision

As soon as is reasonably practicable after the meeting, you must write to the employee to inform him or her of your decision.

You are not required by the Regulations to give a reason for your decision. However, there are strong arguments in favour of indicating to the employee why you have made the particular decision in respect of his or her request. We consider this further at page 38.

The ACAS Guidance expressly acknowledges that you are not required to give a reason. In terms of employee relations, there may be arguments for and against giving a reason for your decision and this is an issue you should consider in each case. We think that it will assist employee relations if you can refer to a retirement policy which sets out the procedural steps and identifies the factors which may be taken into account in deciding on requests. We consider retirement policies in more detail at the end of this chapter.

The only legal consequences of your giving, or not giving, a reason for your decision would arise where your actions could be taken as evidence of discrimination on grounds other than age (for example, sex or disability). If in doubt you should seek the advice of your EEF Association.

The Regulations do impose certain requirements for the decision letter (see Appendix 6 for sample letters), and you must ensure that your decision letter meets these requirements as even minor errors will result in a breach of the procedure:

- The decision must be given in writing, and it must be dated.
- If your decision is to refuse the request, the letter must confirm that you wish the employee to retire and the date on which dismissal will take effect. It must also inform the employee of the right to appeal.
- If your decision is to accept the request, the letter must state that it is accepted. It must also state either that you agree to the employment continuing indefinitely, or that you agree that employment will continue for a specific period and state the length of this period or the date when the period will end.
- If your decision is to allow the employee to continue working but for a shorter period than requested by the employee, the letter must also inform the employee of the right to appeal.

You should always hold the meeting and give your decision before retirement takes effect. If you effect the retirement before giving your decision, then the Regulations provide that the employee's employment continues until the day after you give the decision (although for the purposes of an unfair dismissal claim, the relevant date is that on which retirement actually took effect).

Hold an appeal meeting

If the employee decides to appeal, he or she must write to do so as soon as reasonably practicable. The employee's notice of appeal must be in writing, be dated and set out the grounds of appeal.

On receipt of the appeal letter, you must hold an appeal meeting within a reasonable time. The procedure does not require that a different and/or more senior person holds the appeal meeting from the person who held the first meeting.

The purpose of the meeting is to discuss the appeal. You should therefore ensure that the employee is given a proper opportunity to put forward the grounds of his or her appeal and that these are discussed. Although the procedure does not require you to give a reason for your decision after the first meeting, in practice you may find that you need to inform the employee of the reason so that you can have a proper discussion about his or her appeal.

Inform the employee of your final decision

As soon as is reasonably practicable after the appeal meeting, you must write to the employee to inform him or her of your decision.

The requirements for your final decision letter are the same as for your first decision letter, although of course in this case you do not need to inform the employee of the right to appeal. Again, you are not required to give a reason. Sample decision letters after an appeal are contained in Appendix 6.

Circumstances where you are not required to hold a meeting

There is no requirement under the procedure to hold a meeting or an appeal meeting if you agree with the employee that the employment will continue indefinitely and confirm this by dated letter to the employee. Nor is there a requirement to hold a meeting or appeal meeting if you agree with the employee that employment will continue for an agreed period and you confirm this by dated letter and specify when employment will end.

The Regulations also provide that you do not have to hold the meeting or appeal meeting if it is not practicable to do so within a reasonable period, and you consider the request or appeal by taking into account any representations made by the employee. This could arise, for example, where the employee is unable to attend a meeting because of long-term illness. You must still give the employee written (and dated) notice of your decision as required under the procedure. We do not recommend that you rely on this provision without first seeking the advice of your EEF Association.

Employee's right to be accompanied at meetings

Employees have the right to reasonably request to be accompanied at meetings under this procedure, although they can only be accompanied by a fellow worker and not by an external trade union official or steward. The companion can address the meeting and confer with the employee, but cannot answer questions on the employee's behalf.

If the companion is unavailable to attend the meeting but the employee proposes an alternative time within the next seven calendar days which is convenient for all, then you must postpone the meeting to that time.

A breach by you of this right entitles the employee to complain to an employment tribunal, which may award him or her up to two weeks' pay (subject to the statutory limit on a week's pay, which at the time of writing is £290).

Dealing with a 'second' retirement

Where you have agreed to a request not to retire, it is likely (or indeed it may be certain because you have agreed a fixed period of continued employment) that you will reach a time when, for a second time, you intend the employee to retire.

When you intend the employment to terminate in these circumstances, you are once again under the obligation to follow the procedural steps set out in the Regulations. You should give standard notification, and the employee has the right to request not to retire. If he or she makes a valid request, you have the duty to consider it and follow the procedure.

This means that, if you agree to a request not to retire and agree that the employee will continue for a fixed period of a year or less, then you can give standard notification at the same time as, or soon after, you give your decision on the request.

There is one specific provision in the Regulations which applies where you agree that the employee will continue to work but only for a *fixed period of six months or less*. The effect of this provision is that you are not required to follow the procedural steps again. This is considered in Chapter 7 (see page 44).

Employees due to retire between 1 October 2006 and 31 March 2007

The legislation requires you to give employees you wish to retire at least six months' notification of their intended date of retirement ('the standard notification') – regardless of how much notice they are entitled to under their contract.

What happens though where the intended retirement date falls within the first six months after the Regulations come into force, that is, between 1 October 2006 and 31 March 2007? During this period, there will be insufficient time to give the standard notification. Instead, the basic rule is that you have to give the employee their contractual or statutory notice to expire on their intended retirement date.

Giving notice before 1 October 2006

That rule, however, is modified if, in order to comply, you would have to give notice before 1 October. In such a case, the legislation allows you to give an employee less than their full entitlement to notice, provided that you give them notice before 1 October and that notice is at least four weeks long (and expires on their intended retirement date). At some time before 1 October, you should also inform the employee that they are being retired on the dismissal date.

You should then, on 1 October or, if that is not practicable (1 October 2006 is after all a Sunday), as soon as possible thereafter (normally 2 October), inform the employee in writing of their right to request not to retire.

Although these rules allow you to give at least four weeks' notice rather than contractual notice, we recommend that you give full contractual notice wherever possible. This is because, as you are giving notice of dismissal, the employee may successfully argue that full notice is due.

Giving notice after 1 October

If you give notice after 1 October, you must give the employee their full notice, to expire on the intended date of retirement. At the same time or before (i.e. at any time from 1 October onwards) you must inform the employee in writing of their right to request not to retire.

In either case, if the employee subsequently requests not to retire – at least four weeks before the retirement date or, if that is not practicable, as soon as reasonably practicable (which might be up to four weeks after the retirement) – you must consider the request by following the procedure to consider a request set out above.

You should be aware that long-term sick employees who have exhausted their right to sick pay but whose notice entitlement is to statutory minimum notice will have to be paid their normal pay during their notice period (see page 58).

Note that if you have an employee whom you wish to retire on 1 April 2007, you must give the full six months' notice of their intended date of retirement, i.e. on 1 October 2006.

Considering a request

There are a number of factors you should take into account when you are considering a request by an employee not to retire.

You will of course need to consider each request on its own merits. Your decision will depend not only on the overall strategy you have decided to apply to retirement (see Chapter 5), but also on the needs of the business at the time the request is made and the likely needs in the medium term. For example, there may be a skills shortage or there may be redundancies in the offing.

You should also bear in mind the implications of allowing the employee to continue working beyond retirement age, and check that the arrangements you wish to apply are not unlawful. These issues are considered in Chapter 7.

If you do not want to accept a request, then, provided that the employee is aged 65 or over and the conditions for a 'safe retirement' are met (see Chapter 8), there should be no risk of age discrimination or unfair dismissal in refusing the request and compulsorily retiring the employee.

There are however risks under the other discrimination laws. For example, if the reason you refuse a request is because of the employee's illness, then you may face a claim for disability discrimination. If you refuse the request of a female employee but accept the request of a male employee in comparable circumstances, then she may have grounds for a sex discrimination claim. Your decision to refuse a request should not be based, either directly or indirectly, on grounds of sex, gender, disability, religion or belief or sexual orientation.

You should ensure that requests are dealt with in a way that is non-discriminatory, and also in a way that is perceived to be fair. You will find it easier to manage employees' expectations if you have a written policy on retirement to refer to (see below), and we recommend that you refer to this policy when informing employees of your decision.

Should you give a reason for your decision?

The Regulations do not require you to give a reason for your decision on a request not to retire. However, ACAS recommends that as a matter of good practice, employees should be given a reason and an explanation of the employer's retirement policy. The ACAS guidance states that giving a reason 'may enable the employee to leave with dignity and respect and help you maintain good workplace relationships with other employees'.

The ACAS guidance also reminds employers that, if they are giving a reason, they should be careful not to suggest that they are discriminating against the employee on other grounds, such as disability or sex (we identify above the risks of discrimination on other grounds). This is an important point. The only legal consequences of you giving, or not giving, a reason for your decision would arise where your actions could be taken as evidence of discrimination on grounds other than age. In order to defend a discrimination claim in these circumstances, it will assist you if you have provided the employee with a non-discriminatory reason at the time you made your decision.

With these points in mind, we recommend that you introduce a written retirement policy, which sets out the types of factors which would lead you to allowing employees to continue working beyond retirement. Having such a policy will help to manage employees' expectations about how their requests will be handled. It will also assist you in giving the reasons for your decisions on employees' requests – see further below.

Implementing a retirement policy

A written policy will raise awareness amongst employees of the procedural steps that you are required to follow and assist those who are responsible for implementing these steps. It will also give employees guidance on how their requests will be handled, and assist you in giving reasons for your decisions. We therefore recommend that you put together a written retirement policy. A sample is contained in Appendix 4.

In drawing up a policy, you need to think first about the operational aspects of retirement – that is, the procedural steps. We recommend that you identify who in your organisation has responsibility for sending standard notifications, who has responsibility for holding meetings to discuss requests, who has responsibility for making decisions and for sending out decision letters. Depending on the size of your business, you may wish to allocate these responsibilities between HR (Human Resources) and your line managers. You should then explain the procedural steps in a written policy, so that employees understand what is required of you and of them.

As well as the operational aspect of the procedure, you also need to think about the factors you should take into account in considering requests by employees not to retire. Ask yourself questions such as: do you wish to rigidly enforce retirement at a specific age, or do you want to take a flexible approach? What would be the likely impact of these approaches on your workforce and business needs? Adopting an overall strategy for how you approach retirement (see Chapter 5) will assist you in answering these questions. You should also bear in mind the issues raised in Chapter 7, which looks at the legal implications of agreeing to requests.

There is no one 'right' policy and the approach you take is down to your own business decision. However, we do recommend that whatever your overall strategy, you assess all requests not to retire by reference to certain objective and business-driven criteria and that these are indicated in the written policy. This will assist you in ensuring that decisions on employees' requests are dealt with fairly and without discrimination. It will also enable you to give a reason to the employee for your decision, namely that you are accepting the request because the employee satisfies the criteria, or you are refusing the request because he or she does not satisfy them.

Appendix 4 contains a sample retirement policy which follows these recommendations. It is for use when the employer wishes to enforce a retirement age of 65 unless exceptional circumstances apply. It sets out the procedural steps, and also gives examples of exceptional circumstances which, if they apply, will lead to the employer agreeing to a request by an employee not to retire.

7

Employees working beyond retirement age

In this chapter we deal with some key issues in respect of allowing employees to continue working beyond their retirement age. We consider the terms and conditions you apply to employees working beyond retirement age, the duration of their employment, whether you can impose a break in service, and issues relating to employees who are, at the time the age discrimination legislation comes into force, already working for you beyond retirement age.

Terms and conditions

Before age discrimination legislation was introduced, it was common for employers to issue a fresh contract of employment to those employees they were retaining after their retirement date. Under the new contract, employees may have been excluded from certain benefits. For example, any private medical, life insurance or permanent health insurance (PHI) cover may have been stopped because of the cost of providing them.

The employer may also have excluded such employees from the company pension, severance payment or sick pay schemes (or made eligibility entirely discretionary), due to the perception that it would be inappropriate for them to receive the benefit in circumstances where they could retire and a state or other pension could be payable. Another reason for excluding them from the sick pay scheme was the statutory sick pay (SSP) rule whereby employees over 65 were not normally entitled to be paid SSP, which meant the employer could not offset SSP paid against company sick pay due.

The above are all examples of the pay and benefits of older employees being directly determined by their age.

The general principle is that it is unlawful for you to discriminate against employees on age grounds in the pay and benefits you offer even if the employee is over your retirement age or 65 unless an exemption applies or you can justify the practice. However, as the exemptions assist in a limited way only, you will normally have to justify any differences in treatment between retained employees and those younger than 65 or the retirement age.

We consider specific benefits below.

Life insurance, private health care cover, PHI benefits

You will need to justify excluding older employees from access to these benefits as there is no exemption to cover doing so. This means that, if challenged, you would have to persuade a tribunal that you are not discriminating just because it is cheaper to do so, but because you have a good business reason and there is not another or less discriminatory way of achieving your objective.

For example, it may be so prohibitively expensive to provide PHI benefits to this category of employee that, if you were compelled to provide it for them, you could no longer afford to provide the benefit at all and you would have to remove it from everyone, which would demotivate your workforce. But if, for example:

- the difference in cost to you is relatively marginal compared with the overall cost of providing the benefit to the rest of the workforce and/or the employee's overall remuneration package; or
- there is a possibility of a cost-sharing arrangement with the older employee;

then you may not be able to justify excluding them.

SSP and company sick pay schemes

From 1 October 2006 employees over age 65 are eligible for SSP; the rule excluding them is repealed. For example, if you have an employee aged

66 who starts a period of sick leave on 1 September 2006, they are only eligible for SSP (assuming all the other qualifying rules for it are satisfied) from 1 October 2006. There is no exemption covering a practice of excluding employees over retirement age from your company sick pay scheme.

We think it unlikely you would be able to justify to an employment tribunal continuing with this practice. The legislation effectively requires you to treat such employees in the same way as your younger ones.

Enhanced redundancy pay

The exemption for enhanced redundancy schemes does not cover a policy of excluding employees on age grounds from receiving payment under the scheme.

As we explain in Chapter 9, the upper age limit on the right to claim a statutory redundancy payment has been removed. Against this background, we think it unlikely you would be able to justify excluding employees over retirement age from your enhanced redundancy scheme.

On the other hand, there may be occasions when you have sufficient planning time to follow the required procedural steps for retiring the employee (see Chapter 6) rather than making him or her redundant. You should consider doing so only where the employee is aged 65 or over.

Pensions

Under the pension exemptions you can set a maximum age for admission to your occupational pension scheme. However, if an employee is already a scheme member when you agree to allow them to continue in employment, stopping them from accruing benefits under the scheme will be unlawful unless you can justify it. Chapter 14 deals with pensions in detail.

If you allow an employee to continue working beyond retirement age, you should check with the pension trustees and the pension scheme advisers whether employees will be allowed to draw down their pension benefits even though they are continuing to work for you and, if so, to what extent. (See further Chapter 14.)

Duration of employment

When employees make a request not to retire, they must specify whether they are asking you to retain them after retirement age on an indefinite basis or for a fixed period or until a specified date. If you agree to their request to stay on, you must put in writing the duration you have agreed to. If the period of continued employment is more than six months, then you must follow the procedural steps again if you wish to retire the employee at the end of the fixed period. (For six months or less, see below.)

There is a different consideration if you are *recruiting* an employee who is older than your retirement age, as opposed to allowing an existing employee to continue working after their retirement age. If you placed them from the outset on a fixed-term contract in circumstances when you would not have engaged a younger employee on one, this is likely to amount to discriminatory treatment on grounds of age unless you can justify it. However, following the date on which age discrimination legislation comes into force, there is less of a business requirement to use fixed-term contracts for managing the employment of an older worker as you can follow the procedural steps to retire employees when the need arises.

Agreeing to a short period of continued employment

You may encounter a situation where you want the employee to continue working beyond his or her retirement date, but only for a short period. This can arise, for example, if the employee is needed for a short project, or for a limited hand-over period, or indeed where the employee wants to continue for a short time only.

There is a specific provision in the Regulations which is useful in such circumstances. The provision applies where:

- the employee makes a request not to retire; and
- you agree that he or she can continue working but only for *a fixed period of six months or less*; and
- you give notice to the employee of the date on which the fixed period will end.

The effect of the provision is that you are not required to give standard notification in respect of the deferred retirement (i.e. the end of the fixed period), nor is the employee entitled to make a second request not to retire.

Where you agree to a fixed period of six months or less, you are not required to have a meeting with the employee to discuss the request (although you may choose to do so), provided that you notify the employee of the date on which the fixed period will end.

Provided that you gave standard notification in respect of the first retirement date, and that the employee was aged 65 or over at this first retirement date, then you will be safe from liability for unfair dismissal (see Chapter 8).

Breaks in service

For tax and pension reasons (see Chapter 14), and/or to establish a break in service for statutory or contractual benefits, many employers have in the past insisted on employees having a break in service before continuing to work after retirement age.

Under the age discrimination legislation we think it unlikely you could justify this practice, which is discriminatory on age grounds. If, as a result of it, an employee is paid, for example, a lower amount of sick pay than they would have been if there had been no break in service, they could make a claim to the tribunal that they were disadvantaged on the grounds of their age. The tribunal can award compensation for any benefits that they have lost as a result of the break in service and make an award for injury to feelings.

Employees already working past retirement age

You may already have employees working past their retirement age or age 65 at 1 October 2006 when the legislation comes into force.

If you intend them to retire between 1 October 2006 and 31 March 2007, then you must follow the transitional provisions for compulsorily retiring them (see Chapter 6).

You may also have retained them, before 1 October 2006, on a fixed-term contract or a succession of fixed-term contracts. The same principle applies as if you had retained them on a contract of indefinite duration: when the contract comes up for renewal on or after 1 October 2006 and you intend them to retire, you must follow the procedural steps (or the transitional provisions) as if they were coming up to their original retirement date.

If you retained employees past retirement age on a benefits package that, because of their age, is less favourable than that applying to their younger colleagues, it is likely that a tribunal would allow them to bring age discrimination claims if you continued to maintain any differences in treatment after 1 October 2006 unless you could justify them (see above for further details).

8

Retirement and unfair dismissal

This chapter describes the impact of the age discrimination legislation on the law of unfair dismissal. As highlighted in Chapter 4, the impact is considerable. Here, we cover the following issues:

- the link between retirement and dismissal;
- the removal of the upper age limit to claim unfair dismissal;
- the significance of the 'normal retirement age'; and
- how to avoid unfair dismissal when you retire employees.

In many cases, your employees will want to retire at their retirement age and there will be no question of their wanting to bring a claim of unfair dismissal against you. However, the Regulations make it clear that in certain circumstances, there is the potential for employees to claim unfair dismissal when you have required them to retire.

The provisions on unfair dismissal in the context of retirement are very complex. However, the key message for employers is fairly straightforward:

You will not be liable for unfair dismissal if:

- you retire employees only once they have reached age 65 or a higher normal retirement age; and
- you take the procedural steps set out in Chapter 6, namely giving standard notification and following the procedure for considering a request not to retire.

Link between retirement and dismissal

The age discrimination legislation is based on the premise that to require an employee to retire amounts to dismissal of the employee.

This is because either the employer is unilaterally ending the employment against the employee's wishes or because the contract is a 'limited term contract', the expiry of which is deemed to be a dismissal.

There is some scope to argue about these presumptions. However, the legal arguments over whether retirement amounts to a dismissal need not concern employers in everyday practice. If you use the sample letters in Appendix 6 when following the procedural steps set out in Chapter 6, you will avoid using the terminology of dismissal in retiring the employee and so, at least to some extent, you can mitigate the adverse impact on employee relations of appearing to bring to an end a career by dismissal. You will also avoid the risk of successful unfair dismissal claims, whether or not your actions are found to amount to dismissal.

Removal of the upper age limit

Prior to 1 October 2006, employees were excluded from the right not to be unfairly dismissed if they were aged 65 or over, or if they had reached the employer's normal retirement age or over and that retirement age was the same for men and women. This 'upper age limit' is removed by the age discrimination legislation. Employees of *any* age have the right not to be unfairly dismissed and can bring unfair dismissal claims against their employers.

The significance of the 'normal retirement age'

A key concept in the new provisions on unfair dismissal is the 'normal retirement age' (NRA). The NRA is crucial to the fairness or unfairness of a dismissal brought about by compulsory retirement.

In essence, an employer who compulsorily retires an employee before his or her NRA (even if the NRA is 65 or over) cannot argue in defence of a subsequent unfair dismissal claim that the reason for the dismissal was retirement.

A dismissal before the NRA can be fair only if the employer relies on another reason, such as misconduct or capability, and if it has followed the statutory disciplinary and dismissal procedure if this applies.

It is therefore important that you identify whether or not an employee has an NRA, and if so, what the NRA is. This should be done prior to commencing the procedural steps for retiring the employee.

How do you identify an employee's NRA?

The legislation defines an employee's NRA as 'the age at which employees in the employer's undertaking who hold, or have held, the same kind of position as the employee are normally required to retire'.

The key issue is what happens in reality: when do you normally require employees to retire? Many employees have provisions in their employment contracts that stipulate a specific retirement age. However, this 'contractual retirement age' is not necessarily the same as the NRA. A contractual retirement age may not be conclusive of the NRA because, over the passage of time, the NRA may well become something different. For example, where an employer has stipulated 60 as the retirement age in its employees' contracts of employment, but has in fact allowed all employees to work on until they reach 65, the contractual retirement age is 60 but the NRA is 65.

You should contact your EEF Association for advice if you are in doubt as to the NRA of an employee whom you intend to retire.

Avoiding unfair dismissal when you retire an employee

Retiring an employee is likely to be viewed as dismissing the employee. He or she therefore has a potential unfair dismissal claim. The Regulations introduce new provisions about retirement to the legislation on unfair dismissal (contained in the Employment Rights Act 1996).

Remember that compulsory retirement – one that takes place against the employee's wishes – is likely to amount to a dismissal. It may seem an obvious point, but you should bear in mind that the legal framework we consider below is relevant only where there has indeed been a dismissal. Employees who cannot show that they were retired against their wishes will be unable to succeed in unfair dismissal claims because they will be unable to establish that they were dismissed. In particular, we believe that it will be difficult for an employee who was given standard notification (see Chapter 6), but made no request not to retire, to argue that the retirement was effected against his or her wishes.

The new provisions on unfair dismissal are extremely complex and identify a large number of different scenarios which may or may not result in an unfair dismissal. Here we focus on the points that you as the employer need to know in order to minimise the risk of successful unfair dismissal claims.

It is possible to identify three groups of scenarios in which a compulsory retirement could amount to a fair or unfair dismissal.

1. **Safe retirements.** Under the legislation, there are certain circumstances in which you can compulsorily retire an employee safe in the knowledge that it will be a fair dismissal (what we refer to as 'safe retirements'). Essentially, the retirement must take place when or after the employee reaches age 65 or a higher NRA, and you must also comply with the procedural steps.

> We recommend that you retire employees only in the circumstances of a safe retirement. In essence, this means that you should not attempt to retire employees below their NRA, and in any event below age 65.

2. **Risky retirements.** There is a limited set of circumstances for compulsory retirement at or after age 65 where, although you have not met all the requirements for a safe retirement, you *may* none the less be able to defend an unfair dismissal claim. We refer to this set as 'risky retirements'.

3. **Unfair retirements.** There are situations in which you are prevented by the legislation from arguing that a dismissal was on grounds of retirement. In these situations, if you have treated the dismissal as a retirement, it will almost certainly be unfair dismissal because you will not have followed the appropriate procedure. We therefore refer to them as 'unfair retirements'. These situations include early retirement, retirement at an NRA that is lower than 65 and not justified, and dismissal before the intended date of retirement.

   We now consider each group in more detail.

Safe retirements

The legislation identifies certain circumstances in which you as the employer are protected from liability for unfair dismissal.

The circumstances for a safe retirement are as follows:

- Employment must terminate when the employee has reached the NRA or is over this age, provided that the NRA is 65 or higher.
- If there is no NRA, employment must terminate when the employee has reached age 65 or over.
- You must have given standard notification.
- If the employee made a valid request not to retire, you must have followed the procedure to consider it.
- Employment must terminate on the date which you specified in the standard notification as the intended date of retirement.
- If you compulsorily retire an employee in these circumstances, it will be a fair dismissal.

Examples

The employee's NRA is 67. His 67th birthday is on 10 December. The employer gave him the standard notification between twelve and six months before this date. He made a request not to retire and the employer followed the procedure to consider it, but refused the request. Employment terminated on 10 December.

The employee has no NRA. Between twelve and six months before his 65th birthday, the employer gave him the standard notification that it intended him to retire on his 65th birthday. He made no request not to retire. Employment terminated on his 65th birthday.

The employee has an NRA of 65. However, she continued to work past this age. Between twelve and six months before her 68th birthday, the employer gave her the standard notification that it intended her to retire on her 68th birthday. She made a request not to retire and the employer followed the procedure to consider it, but refused the request. Employment terminated on her 68th birthday.

The legislation sets out one other set of circumstances in this category. This is where the employee has an NRA which is under 65 but is justified, and compulsory retirement takes place when the employee reaches the NRA or is over this age. The other elements must also be satisfied: you must have given standard notification, followed the procedure to consider a request if one was made, and employment must terminate on the date specified in the standard notification. Although these circumstances amount to a fair retirement, they are unlikely to apply very often because of the difficulty of justifying a retirement age lower than 65 (see Chapter 5). Moreover, if the NRA cannot be justified, the retirement falls into the category of 'unfair retirements' and you run a high risk of liability for unfair dismissal.

Risky retirements

If you effect a compulsory retirement in circumstances that do not fall within those set out above for a safe retirement, then the likelihood is that you will be unable to defend a claim for unfair dismissal.

However, there are two very limited exceptions. These are where the compulsory retirement meets the circumstances for a safe retirement but:

- you gave fall-back notification instead of standard notification; or
- the employee's employment terminated later than the intended date of retirement specified in the standard notification.

Examples

The employee's NRA is 67. His 67th birthday is on 10 December. The employer failed to give standard notification, but gave fall-back notification three months before this date. The employee made a request not to retire and the employer followed the procedure to consider it, but refused the request. Employment terminated on 10 December.

The employee has no NRA. The employer failed to give standard notification, but gave the employee fall-back notification four months in advance of his 65th birthday that it intended him to retire on his 65th birthday. He made no request not to retire. Employment terminated on his 65th birthday.

The employee has an NRA of 65. However, she continued to work past this age. Between twelve and six months before her 68th birthday, the employer gave her the standard notification and specified that the intended date of retirement was her 68th birthday. She made a request not to retire and the employer followed the procedure to consider it, but refused the request. For payroll reasons, employment terminated two weeks after her 68th birthday.

In these circumstances, you may be able to establish that the compulsory retirement was a fair dismissal, but you will first have to persuade the tribunal that the reason for the dismissal was retirement rather than another reason. The closer you have adhered to the procedural steps for retirement, the more likely you are to prove that retirement was the reason for the dismissal.

If you can prove that the reason was retirement, your second step is to show that the dismissal was fair. You can only do this if, at the minimum, you gave fall-back notification and complied with the procedure for considering a request if one was made.

Unfair retirements

The legislation identifies certain circumstances in which you cannot argue before an employment tribunal that the reason for dismissal was retirement, even if you treated it as a retirement and followed the procedural steps. These circumstances are early retirements, retirement at an NRA lower than 65 that is not justified and dismissal before the intended date of retirement.

In these circumstances, you cannot use retirement as the grounds for defending an unfair dismissal claim.

Instead, to ensure that you dismiss fairly, you must identify another reason – conduct, capability, redundancy, illegality or some other substantial reason – as the reason for dismissal, and ensure that you meet the relevant standards of fairness. This may also require you to follow the statutory dismissal and disciplinary procedure, if it applies (see the EEF Guide *Dispute Resolution, A Practical Guide to the New Law*).

The effect of these provisions is that you must identify the correct reason well in advance of the dismissal, so that you handle it appropriately. The circumstances where you need to do this are considered below.

Early retirement

You cannot argue that the reason for dismissal was retirement where:

- employment terminates before the employee reaches the NRA; or
- there is no NRA and employment terminates before the employee reaches age 65.

Clearly, this means that there are significant risks in compulsorily retiring employees earlier than when they reach age 65 or earlier than their NRA (even if the NRA is higher than 65).

If you are considering imposing early retirement on an employee, you must *not* follow the procedure for retirement. You must identify in advance what the reason is for terminating the employment – conduct, capability, redundancy, illegality or some other substantial reason. You must then ensure that dismissal is fair in the circumstances, given the reason you have identified. You must also follow the statutory dismissal and disciplinary procedure if this applies. If in doubt you should seek advice from your EEF Association.

Examples

The employee is on long-term sickness absence. He is 61, and his NRA is 65. If the employer wishes to terminate his employment before his 65th birthday, it must identify another reason for this, most likely capability. It must ensure that dismissal is fair in the circumstances, and it must follow the statutory dismissal and disciplinary procedure. (It must also be aware of its obligations under disability discrimination legislation.) If the employer instead followed the procedural steps for retirement, or no procedure at all, the dismissal would be unfair.

The employee has no NRA. He is 64. A redundancy situation arises, and the employee's job is at risk. To terminate his employment, the employer must identify redundancy as the reason for the dismissal. It must ensure that the dismissal is fair in the circumstances, for example by using objective selection criteria, consulting with the employee and looking for any suitable alternative employment. It must also follow the statutory dismissal and disciplinary procedure (unless it does not apply because it is a redundancy of 20 employees or more). If the employer decided instead to follow the procedural steps for retirement, the dismissal would be unfair.

Remember that the unfair dismissal provisions apply only where there is a dismissal, i.e. a termination of employment contrary to the employee's wishes. Where the employee instigates the early retirement, or where you are certain that you have the employee's agreement to it, then the employee is unlikely to be able to establish that he or she was dismissed. You may therefore decide not to follow any procedure, although we recommend at the least that you obtain written confirmation from them that their employment is terminating by mutual agreement or at their instigation.

Retirement at NRA lower than 65

If an employee's NRA is lower than 65 and you cannot justify it (see Chapter 5), then you cannot argue that the reason for dismissing the employee at or after that age was retirement even if you treated it as such.

We have already warned in Chapter 5 of the difficulties of justifying lower retirement ages. This provision of the legislation increases the potential liability that you face if you have an NRA of under 65.

Dismissal before the intended date of retirement

You cannot argue that the reason for dismissal was retirement where:

- you gave standard notification but employment terminates earlier than the intended date of retirement (regardless of whether the employee was above or below the NRA/age 65); or
- you gave fall-back notification but employment terminates earlier than the intended date of retirement (regardless of whether the employee was above or below the NRA/age 65).

Essentially, these provisions prevent employers from using retirement as a means of avoiding dismissing the employee for another reason, such as conduct or capability.

Examples

The employee's 65th birthday is 1 August. The employer gives standard notification which specifies that the intended date of retirement is 1 August. However, in May the employee commits an act of gross misconduct. If the employer simply brings forward the date of dismissal to May but claims that this it is retiring the employee, the dismissal will be unfair. For a fair dismissal before the intended date of retirement, the employer must follow the statutory dismissal and disciplinary procedure and ensure that dismissal for misconduct is fair in all the circumstances.

The employee's NRA is 67 and her 67th birthday is 31 March. The employer forgot to give standard notification, but gave fall-back notification which specified that the intended date of retirement is 31 March. However, a redundancy situation arises in February and the employee's job is at risk. If the employer simply brings forward the date of dismissal to February but claims that it is retiring the employee, the dismissal will be unfair. For a fair dismissal before the intended date of retirement, the employer must follow the statutory dismissal and disciplinary procedure (if applicable) and ensure that dismissal for redundancy is fair in all the circumstances.

Again, remember that you face liability only if there has in fact been a dismissal. If the employee agrees to the termination of his or her employment earlier than the retirement date, then you may escape liability because the employment terminates by mutual agreement instead of being a dismissal. This is also the case if the employee resigns earlier than the intended retirement date. But there is always a risk if no procedure is followed and we recommend that you seek advice from your EEF Association in these circumstances.

Can the employee claim wrongful dismissal?

Does the employee have a wrongful dismissal claim in respect of compulsory retirement, i.e. a claim for notice?

The requirement to give notice only applies in respect of dismissal. If an employee voluntarily retires on the retirement date, then the termination of his or her employment at that time is unlikely to amount to a dismissal. But where retirement is brought about against the employee's wishes, he or she may argue that the retirement was a dismissal and claim that they are entitled to contractual or statutory notice.

We take the view that the sample standard notification contained in Appendix 5 includes wording which is sufficient to give notice. This is because it is addressed personally to the employee and it informs them of when their employment will terminate (subject to any agreement reached in the event that the employee makes a request). Provided that you give the employee standard notification in sufficient time to cover their notice period – and this will be the case for most employees, unless they have very long contractual notice periods – then we believe you should have a defence to any action for wrongful dismissal (i.e. dismissal without notice).

Retiring employees on long-term sickness absence

You may face a situation where an employee has been on long-term sickness absence and has exhausted the right to company sick pay. There is a provision in employment legislation that entitles an employee who is dismissed in these circumstances, and who is entitled at most to statutory notice plus 6 days, to normal pay for their period of notice.

Employees in these circumstances have a potential claim for notice pay if, in the absence of a contractual retirement age, you compulsorily retire them.

As with all employees whom you intend to retire, where an employee on long-term sickness absence reaches his or her NRA or age 65 and you wish them to retire, you should give them standard notification and ensure that you follow the other procedural steps.

9

Redundancy

This chapter considers:

- the impact of the age discrimination legislation on statutory redundancy payments;
- enhanced payments; and
- selection for redundancy and volunteers.

At the end of the chapter, we give advice in respect of reviewing your redundancy policies or practices.

Employees' ages have long been a relevant factor in redundancy situations. Age is taken into account in the calculation of an employee's statutory redundancy payment, and can also determine the amount of an enhanced redundancy payment made by the employer. Depending on the ages of the employees involved, age can also be relevant where the employer uses length of service to calculate an enhanced redundancy payment, or where length of service is used in the method of selecting employees for redundancy.

Statutory redundancy payments

The basic framework of the scheme for statutory redundancy payments remains in place from 1 October 2006.

In order to qualify for entitlement to a statutory redundancy payment, the employee must have two years' service or more at the time they are dismissed by reason of redundancy. The age bands used to calculate the amount of the payment remain, as do the 'multipliers' of a week's pay in each age band. These are:

- 1.5 weeks' pay for each year of continuous employment in which the employee was aged 41 and over;
- 1 week's pay for each year of employment in which the employee was aged 22 to 40;
- 0.5 week's pay for each year of employment in which the employee was aged 21 and under.

The maximum number of years that can be taken into account is 20. The amount of a week's pay is subject to a statutory limit, which is reviewed annually each February and at the time of writing is £290.

What has changed?

The age discrimination legislation has introduced the following changes to the statutory scheme:

- Employees aged under 18, and 65 and over, are no longer excluded from entitlement to a statutory redundancy payment.
- The 'tapering rule' for employees dismissed after their 64th birthday (whereby the payment is reduced by one-twelfth for each month elapsed between the birthday and dismissal) has been removed.
- The rules that allow the statutory redundancy payment to be offset against the benefit of a pension (to which the employee is entitled immediately after dismissal) have been removed.

It is clear that the statutory scheme continues to rely on the age of the particular employee in order to calculate the amount of the statutory redundancy payment. The government believes that the use of the age bands (41 and over, 22 to 40, 21 and under) is justified on the basis of the increasing difficulties faced by older employees in obtaining a new job after being dismissed on grounds of redundancy. Since this scheme is a statutory one, employers are legally obliged to follow it and cannot breach the Regulations as a result.

At the time of writing, certain trade unions and interest groups do not share the government's view and intend to lodge a legal challenge against the statutory redundancy scheme on the basis that it does not comply with the Directive's provisions on age discrimination. If the challenge were to succeed, this would require the government to remove the statutory scheme and introduce a different one. This would have a knock-on effect for employers' enhanced schemes because the exemptions for mirror schemes (see below) would also have to be removed. You should seek advice from your EEF Association for up-to-date information on this matter.

Enhanced redundancy pay

Employers often make additional payments to employees to enhance or 'top up' their statutory redundancy payments. The basis for the enhancement varies enormously. Common examples are:

- doubling the amount of the statutory redundancy payment;
- using the employee's actual pay rather than the statutory limit;
- applying a percentage increase to the statutory redundancy payment depending on the employee's age; and
- adding an additional sum depending on the employee's age or length of service.

In the context of age discrimination, the vital issue is whether the basis for the enhancement relies to any extent on the age of the employee. If the enhancement is determined by direct reference to the employee's age, or indirectly by reference to the employee's length of service, then there is a risk that it will fall foul of the age discrimination legislation.

> However, not all age-related enhanced schemes are rendered unlawful by the legislation. The Regulations contain a specific exemption for enhanced schemes that mirror the statutory redundancy payments scheme.

The status of the scheme – whether it is an express contractual entitlement, a matter of custom and practice, a one-off or an *ex gratia* payment – is immaterial for these purposes.

Exemption for corresponding schemes

The Regulations contain an exemption for enhanced redundancy payments which are calculated on the same basis as statutory redundancy payments. By virtue of the exemption, employers can do *one or more* of the following without liability for age discrimination:

- Employers can remove the statutory limit on a week's pay, or use a different (higher) limit.
- Employers can 'multiply the multiplier', provided that this is done uniformly for all age bands. For example, an employer can pay one week's pay for age 18 and under, two weeks' pay for age 22–41 and three weeks' pay for age 41 and over (i.e. double the multiplier in each age band).
- Employers can multiply the statutory redundancy payments. For example, an employer can pay double or triple the statutory redundancy payment.
- Employers can make redundancy payments to employees with less than two years' service, provided that the method of calculation is the same as or corresponds to the statutory scheme.

If you as the employer are making enhanced redundancy payments, bear in mind that you can rely on the exemption in the Regulations only if you apply the same enhancement to all employees being made redundant at that time. You can, however, make different enhancements in respect of different redundancy exercises and rely on the exemption if the enhancements correspond to the statutory scheme.

There may be circumstances where you do not apply the same enhancement to all employees in the same redundancy exercise. This might be the case where you have a group of employees whose employment transferred to you under TUPE (Transfer of Undertakings: Protection of Employment) and who are entitled to different terms and conditions in relation to enhanced redundancy payments. In such a case, if an employee made an age discrimination claim on the basis that he or she received a lesser payment than an employee of another age group, then you could not rely on the exemption even if the enhancement corresponded to the statutory scheme. You would instead have to consider justification, as below.

Schemes which do not fall within the exemption

If your enhanced scheme does not fall within the exemption, but does rely on employees' age or length of service, then you may be able to establish that it is lawful if it meets the test of justification (see Chapter 3).

Whether you can meet the test of justification will depend on the particular scheme you are using, the reasons why you are using it and all the relevant circumstances. One difficulty you may face in justifying the scheme is that a tribunal may decide that it is not proportionate because there are viable, and obvious, alternatives: namely, enhanced schemes which are based on the statutory scheme.

Clearly a scheme which falls within the exemption is less vulnerable to challenge than one which is not covered. Provided that there is no successful legal challenge to the statutory scheme (see page 61), then you may wish to consider replacing your scheme with a corresponding scheme so that you can be certain that it is lawful. You should seek further advice from your EEF Association in this regard.

Selection for redundancy

Certain methods and criteria used to select employees for redundancy are linked directly or indirectly to their age. We set these out below and consider the implications of the age discrimination legislation.

Last in, first out (LIFO)

Some employers, often by virtue of a collective agreement, use LIFO as the sole criterion for redundancy selection. LIFO is an objective and transparent method of selecting for redundancy and it is frequently regarded by employers and employees alike as a 'felt fair' method.

LIFO does, however, present difficulties in the context of age discrimination, because it has the potential to treat one age group of employees less favourably than those of another age group. In many workforces, it is quite likely that the older the employee, the longer his or her service is. In such workforces, the application of LIFO puts younger employees at a disadvantage in comparison with older employees.

In our view, if you use LIFO to select for redundancy, and there is a difference in ages between short- and long-serving employees in your workforce, then you risk unlawfully discriminating on grounds of age because it will be difficult to meet the test of justification.

That said, you may have reasons why you want to use or keep using LIFO. We therefore set out at the end of this chapter the arguments which may assist you in trying to establish justification for using LIFO. If you decide to use LIFO for redundancy selection (which, as highlighted above, is a risky strategy), then we recommend that you assess and document your justification at the time you make this decision.

If you are considering moving away from LIFO, you should refer to the section below on changing your redundancy policy.

Length of service in a matrix or as a tie-breaker

Length of service is often used not as the sole criterion for redundancy selection (see LIFO above) but as one of a number of criteria in a matrix, or as a 'tie-breaker' where employees' scores on the other criteria are equal. The ACAS guidance states that using length of service in any selection criteria (and using LIFO) is likely to be age discriminatory, but we believe this oversimplifies the issue.

Where scores are equal and length of service is the determining factor in making the selection, this will place the younger employees in the pool at a disadvantage in comparison with older employees, if overall the younger employees have less service than older employees. In such circumstances, the use of length of service in this way must be justified to avoid unlawful discrimination on grounds of age.

Similar arguments will apply to justifying length of service as apply to justifying LIFO (see the end of this chapter). However, where length of service has been demonstrated to be the only differentiating factor because it is used as a tie-breaker or is the determining factor in a matrix, it should be easier for the employer to establish justification. Using length of service in this way is more likely to be proportionate because of the lack of viable alternative methods to select for redundancy in a fair and objective manner.

Until there is case law on this point, there can be no definitive answer to whether using length of service in this way is justified and therefore not unlawful age discrimination. However, in our view, where the employer uses a number of objective and fair criteria and length of service is the determining factor, then the justification test should be met.

Other age-related criteria for redundancy selection

Using age itself, or nearness to retirement age, as a criterion is unlikely to be justified because there are viable alternatives which are non- or less discriminatory.

Performance

Performance is a common criterion for redundancy selection. However, you should bear in mind any potential differences in the way that older and younger employees' performance is assessed. Older employees may score higher because their performance has not been as closely managed as that of younger employees.

When using performance as part of the selection matrix, you should check that performance has been assessed in a consistent and objective way for all employees regardless of their age. Performance management is considered in Chapter 13.

Pools for selection

The pool of workers identified as at risk of redundancy, and from which selection is made, may in certain circumstances have the potential to be age discriminatory. For example, your workforce may contain a number of fixed-term employees who are generally younger than the permanent employees who do the same work.

If you make the distinction between the fixed-term and permanent employees and only put the former into a pool for selection, then you run the risk of indirect age discrimination (as well as a potential breach of the legislation concerning equal treatment of fixed-term employees). Singling out a particular group of individuals whose ages differ from other groups runs the risk of an age discrimination claim.

Volunteers for redundancy

If you have a practice of calling for volunteers, or if you are considering doing so, you should check whether employees of a certain age could be placed at a disadvantage and if so, you should assess whether the practice will meet the test of justification.

If you place age-related conditions on who can volunteer, then you may face a claim by an employee who was precluded from volunteering on age-related grounds and who was subsequently made redundant compulsorily. If you are considering such a practice, you should seek the advice of your EEF Association.

Employers sometimes also offer an enhanced redundancy package to volunteers which treats employees of a certain age group more, or less, favourably. If you do so, you may be able to rely on the exemption for corresponding schemes if you calculate the enhancement in the prescribed way (see above). This is because the exemption specifically covers paying enhanced redundancy payments only to volunteers.

However, the exemption does not apply if you pay enhancements calculated in different ways to employees made redundant in the same redundancy exercise. If you cannot rely on the exemption, then you will have to assess whether the additionally enhanced payments (for example, a greater enhancement to volunteers) are justified.

Volunteers for early retirement

Although less common now in the climate of struggling pension funds, employers may sometimes call for volunteers to take early retirement with an occupational pension in order to avoid a redundancy dismissal or to reduce the number of compulsory redundancies in the workforce in general. In doing so, they are treating younger employees less favourably than older ones. For example, if early retirement is available for employees aged 55 and over, an employee aged 50 cannot benefit from this and may face dismissal with a statutory redundancy payment only, whereas an employee aged 55 could take early retirement and start to draw his pension.

If certain conditions are met (see Chapter 14), you may be able to rely on a specific pensions exemption as a defence to a claim by the younger employee. If not, you will have to consider whether you can justify the practice of calling for volunteers for early retirement in a redundancy situation. Here, it is important to consider alternative means to reduce the number of compulsory redundancies. If you are facing a redundancy situation and considering calling for early retirement volunteers, you should first consider alternatives such as calling for ordinary volunteers (without age or service conditions), and other means such as reducing overtime and short-time working. The process of assessing justification should always be documented.

Another potential problem that arises in respect of early retirement in a redundancy situation stems from the provisions on unfair dismissal (see Chapter 8). If employment terminates before the employee reaches age 65 or the normal retirement age, then the employer cannot argue that the retirement was the reason why employment terminated.

In most circumstances, an employee who volunteered for early retirement in a redundancy situation would not be considered as having been dismissed by the employer and so unfair dismissal claims are not an issue. However, there have been cases where employees have established that they were dismissed because they had not truly consented to retire, but were in reality being made redundant with a pension (in circumstances where the employer has essentially presented the employee with a stark choice of 'retire or be dismissed for redundancy').

If the tribunal finds that the retirement was not a mutually agreed termination of employment but rather a dismissal, then you risk being held liable for the dismissal. To reduce this risk, we advise that you take steps to ensure that the employee is genuinely volunteering to retire early. The EEF Guide *Handling Redundancies, A Practical Guide to Managing the Legal Issues* suggests further steps you can take (see page 20 of that Guide). If you have any doubts about the employee's willingness to take early retirement, you should seek the advice of your EEF Association to ensure that you follow the correct procedure.

Other terms and practices that relate to age

Some employers, when making enhanced redundancy payments, inform the employees that they are not entitled to be re-employed by the employer within a certain period after the redundancy. A problem arises in this respect only if the employees who are made redundant are of a particular age group – for example, if the employer has used length of service as the sole criterion for selection and younger employees have been selected in preference to older ones.

Here, younger employees have not only been made redundant but also prevented from obtaining new employment with the same employer. In this scenario, there is a risk that an age discrimination claim could succeed, especially if the employer is a significant one in the region or the employee's skills are very specialised and there are limited opportunities for them. It would be difficult to justify the practice because the only aim of the employer relates to cost, and the discriminatory effects of the practice far outweigh any benefit to the employer.

If you are considering applying this type of practice, you should check whether it could result in a disadvantage being suffered by employees of a particular age group. If so, you should avoid using it.

Reviewing your redundancy policy/practice

In light of the issues raised in this chapter, we recommend that you review your practices concerning redundancy and assess whether or not they comply with the Regulations. For example, you should:

- Check whether or not your scheme for making enhanced redundancy payments is covered by the exemption or is justified in any event.
- Monitor the age profile of those provisionally selected for redundancy.
- Monitor the age profile of those who left as volunteers, and whether the package for voluntary redundancy treats employees of a certain age more or less favourably.
- Assess whether the system for selection for redundancy has the potential to discriminate on grounds of age, and if so, whether it can be justified.

You may decide that certain practices run the risk of breaching the age discrimination legislation, and if so, you should think about how to implement a change. The practice may form part of the employees' contractual entitlements: it may be incorporated by collective agreement, or implied as a result of custom and practice, or be expressly incorporated through a contractual policy. In such circumstances, you should be aware of the considerations involved in changing terms and conditions. See the 'Change and reorganisation' section of the EEF Employment Guide (www.employmentguide.org.uk) or contact your EEF Association.

There are also employment relations implications of changing your redundancy practices. In particular, there may be a trade union or employee representative body which is keen to maintain practices such as LIFO, or an enhanced redundancy payments scheme that favours older workers. In negotiating changes to such practices, it is useful to highlight the provisions of the Regulations and the importance of avoiding unlawful age discrimination.

Chapter 11 raises some broader issues in respect of handling unlawful practices.

Can you justify using LIFO for redundancy selection?

To assess whether you can meet the justification test, you first need to identify what your aim is in using LIFO and whether this is a legitimate aim. You must then assess whether using LIFO is a proportionate means to meet this aim.

What are your aims in using LIFO?

Possible aims are:

- **Fairness.** You may use LIFO because you consider it to be the fairest and most objective method of selecting for redundancy, and the one least vulnerable to challenge.
- **Employment relations.** You may use LIFO as the selection method because this has been agreed (perhaps many years ago) with the trade union, and because a departure from LIFO would cause employment relations problems.
- **Cost.** Your reason may be one of cost: shorter-serving employees will be entitled to smaller redundancy payments and so their selection for redundancy will cost you less than the selection of long-serving employees.
- **Objective selection.** You may use LIFO because it is an effective way to distinguish between employees. This could apply, for example, to a group of unskilled manual workers whose performance, attendance and disciplinary records are all very similar but their length of service differs. As we know from unfair dismissal law, the method of selection must be objective, and using length of service is regarded as an objective and fair criterion on which to make a selection.

Are these aims legitimate?

As discussed in Chapter 3, if your sole aim is to save cost, this cannot be used as justification. Wider economic considerations may give you sufficient justification, for example where you could show that the company would risk insolvency if it had to pay bigger redundancy payments. But if your only aim in using LIFO is to save money, then you will not be able to meet the justification test.

You can, however, put cost into the balance along with other aims which correspond to reasonable business needs, such as achieving fairness, maintaining good employment relations and making an objective selection. Any of these aims you rely on must be backed up with evidence to show that their achievement is indeed assisted by the use of LIFO to select for redundancy. For example, you may be able to point to the fact that the trade union or employee representative body agreed to using LIFO, and point to the decisions of courts and tribunals which hold that length of service is an objective factor for redundancy selection.

Is using LIFO a proportionate means of achieving your aims?

The main difficulty here is that there may be other viable alternatives to LIFO that are less discriminatory and also considered to be fair and objective ways to select for redundancy. The use of a selection matrix, which assesses factors such as performance and skill level, attendance and disciplinary records, is common amongst employers and in many circumstances this presents a less discriminatory method of selecting for redundancy whilst also achieving a result that is considered by employer and employees to be fair.

Therefore, we think it will be difficult to meet the test of justification for using LIFO unless there are compelling employment relations reasons and there is no viable alternative method of objective selection. If the use of LIFO cannot be justified, it amounts to unlawful discrimination on grounds of age.

10

Pay and benefits

In this chapter we:

- identify the pay and benefit practices that may be affected by the age discrimination legislation; and
- explain how the special exemptions for pay and benefits apply.

We deal first with pay and benefits which are based on length of service, and then pay and benefits which are based directly on age.

Pay and benefits related to length of service

The Regulations contain provisions which are intended to safeguard pay and benefits that are related to length of service. The effect of these provisions is as follows:

- A special test applies for justifying pay or benefits based on length of service. The test is that it reasonably appears to the employer that the way it uses length of service to determine eligibility for, or the amount of, pay or benefits fulfils a business need. This is an easier test to meet than the usual test of justification under the Regulations (explained in Chapter 3). This is commonly referred to as the length of service exemption.
- The situation is even more straightforward if the pay or benefit is based on length of service of five years or less. The Regulations expressly

provide that it is not unlawful for employers to award lesser pay or benefits on service of that timescale.

Example

You increase sick pay entitlement after one, two, five and ten years' service. Your practice in awarding increases at one, two and five years is automatically protected because the length of service required is five years or less. You will need to consider what business need is fulfilled by the additional increase at ten years' service.

It is important to note that these provisions do not cover pay or benefits awarded on termination of employment, such as severance payments and redundancy payments. Redundancy pay is dealt with in Chapter 9.

Remember, an employee can succeed with an age discrimination complaint based on the way you use length of service only if they can show that their age group is disadvantaged by your practice.

The most obvious case is where your shorter-serving employees tend to be younger. For example, if employees need ten years' service to gain full company sick pay entitlement, none of your employees under 25 will have that entitlement. Your policy has a disproportionate impact on your under-25-year-olds. If the majority of your new recruits tend to be under 35, the policy will also impact disproportionately on the under-35s in your workforce.

Note, also, your practices are covered by these provisions only if you calculate service in accordance with the Regulations. To prevent employers calculating, for example, 'five years' unfairly, so that, in practice, employees need more than five years' service to qualify for a benefit, the legislation sets some minimum standards. If you calculate length of service differently, then the exemption will not apply and you will have to justify the practice in question according to the usual test of justification (see Chapter 3). The rules on calculating service are set out at the end of this chapter.

Where the service required is five years or less

It is quite common for employers to make entitlement to pay or benefits conditional upon a relatively short period of service. Examples are:

- paying enhanced maternity pay provided that the employee has at least one year's service when she starts maternity leave;
- increasing entitlement to company sick pay once the employee has two years' service;
- awarding an extra day of holiday once the employee has two years' service.

All of the above practices are lawful because the employees do not need more than five years' service to qualify for the benefit.

Where service required is over five years

If your employees need more than five years' service to qualify for a particular level of pay or a benefit, and a younger employee who has insufficient service to qualify brings a tribunal claim seeking the same pay or benefits as an employee who qualifies, then you may be able to rely on the special test of justification to defend the claim.

That test requires you to satisfy the tribunal that it reasonably appeared to you that using length of service in the way you do fulfils a business need. The Regulations give some examples of business needs: to reward experience or to encourage loyalty or motivation.

The government clearly intends that employers should be able to justify pay and benefits based on length of service more easily than under the usual test of justification (see Chapter 3). It seems, for example, that an employment tribunal will find that you have met this test even if it considers there is an alternative or less discriminatory method of meeting your business need (which would mean that you would not meet the usual test).

The test does, however, require the employer to make a judgement as to the purpose and effect of linking the award of the benefit to reaching a particular length of service. For example, if your aim was to encourage loyalty but there is no evidence that the benefit was effective to that end (for example, because your labour turnover has remained persistently high for years), a tribunal *may* conclude that it could not reasonably have appeared to you that using length of service in the way you do encouraged loyalty.

Risk assessment

In our view, many employers who use length of service to determine eligibility for benefits will not face a legal challenge to their practices for a number of reasons, not least that these benefits can be popular with employees.

Also, many employees will not think there is anything intrinsically unfair in having to serve time for 'long-service' benefits such as a one-off service award or perhaps even an extra day's leave, as long as the benefit is a modest one and all employees affected could qualify eventually for it.

Many such benefits have been negotiated with trade unions, which may be reluctant to support challenges to them (although the fact that they have been negotiated does not provide you with an automatic defence if there is a legal challenge).

We suggest the practices most likely to be challenged are:

- very long incremental pay-scales; and
- setting a long qualifying period for premium benefits, such as access to beneficial pension schemes, PHI benefits, a generous sick pay entitlement or private health care cover.

None the less, you should examine *any* service-related benefits where service longer than five years is required and decide what business need is fulfilled by tying the award to service. You will need to decide whether to continue with your practice where you have no evidence that there is any business benefit from it.

Rules for calculating length of service

You can rely on the length of service exemption only if the way that you calculate service complies with the approach set out in the Regulations.

There are two options set out in the legislation:

- taking into account total service working for you (including time with an associated employer); or
- taking into account only the length of time the employee has been doing work at a particular level or above, (for example, the time the employee has been in a managerial grade). You must consider the demands made on your workers in terms of, for example, effort, skill and decision-making when you are deciding whether the jobs the employee has done are at the same level or above.

You do not have to choose just one of these approaches. For example, you may choose the first one in calculating length of service for a 'long-service award' but the second option in deciding who is eligible for permanent health insurance benefit. However, in either case, you must disregard whether someone has been working for you part-time or full-time – it is actual service that counts.

Periods of absence

In calculating length of service under either approach, you can exclude periods of absence unless in all the circumstances it would not be reasonable for you to do so. For example, if you generally include periods of absence, it would not be reasonable to single out some individuals to exclude their absence. Nor would it be reasonable to exclude time off granted by other legislation (family leave, public duties, etc.), which, in any event, would render you liable for treating them less favourably because they took leave.

Discounting service prior to an absence

You can also exclude a period of service before the absence if, in all the circumstances, it is reasonable to do so. The relevant circumstances include:

- the length of and the reason for the absence;
- the effect the absence had on the employee's ability to do their duties (for example, if they were away for so long that, when they returned, you had to retrain them and so it might be reasonable to start the clock at zero again for accruing benefits); and

- the way in which you treat other employees' absences in similar circumstances.

Statutory continuity of employment

In relation to absences from work, many employers follow the statutory rules for calculating continuous employment for redundancy payments purposes when assessing length of service for access to various benefits. Broadly speaking, this means counting periods of absence from work towards total service if the employee remains contractually in your employment during the absence. This method of calculating service is likely to be regarded as reasonable, save in one important respect. Unfortunately, it does not follow that ignoring periods of service prior to an absence that breaks continuity of employment will be regarded as reasonable by the tribunal. Treating someone as a new starter after an absence that breaks continuity is not automatically reasonable; it depends on the factors in the previous paragraph.

Remember that if you cannot rely on the service exemptions because of your calculation method, it will be because the tribunal has found it to be unreasonable in some respect. It is likely to be very difficult to persuade a tribunal that, none the less, your practice is justifiable.

New benefit packages for new recruits

Where, to maintain competitiveness, you have had to introduce lesser terms and conditions for new recruits, longer-serving employees will have better terms than these recent recruits. However, service is not the criterion for being awarded the better terms; no matter how long new recruits serve they will never be awarded those terms. As with the case where you 'red circle' existing employees' pay and benefits, however (see Chapter 11) the longer you preserve the differential, the more it will be the case that those on the better terms are older than those on the lesser terms.

This could give rise to indirect age discrimination claims challenging the practice of continuing to award better terms and conditions to those recruited before the relevant date. We address this in Chapter 11.

Pay and benefits based on age

If entitlement to benefits, or the level of wages or salaries you pay, is determined by your workers' actual age, your practice is discriminatory. It is unlawful unless:

- You can rely on an exemption in the legislation; or
- You can justify the practice by showing that it is a proportionate means of achieving a legitimate aim (see Chapter 3). This means persuading a tribunal that you are not discriminating just because it is cheaper to do so but because you have a good business reason and there is not another or less discriminatory way of achieving it.

In practice, it is quite unusual for employers to use age as a criterion for determining whether a worker is entitled to a certain benefit, or for determining the amount of pay or the level of benefit. However, examples can still be found, including in the operation of pension schemes (see Chapter 14) and levels of pay for young workers.

The Regulations contain an exemption for certain pay rates for workers aged 21 and under which are linked to the structure of the national minimum wage. We consider the scope of this exemption below. There is no exemption to cover pay rates of older workers. Although in theory an employer who determines the pay of older workers by reference to their age could seek to justify this practice, in reality this would be extremely difficult. Therefore, in our view, the age discrimination legislation effectively outlaws age-related pay for workers aged 22 or over.

Also, apart from the pension exemptions (see Chapter 14), there is no specific exemption covering a practice of *excluding* workers, young or old, from entitlement to particular benefits, which means that, if challenged, you would have to justify the practice. We consider the implications of this for retaining employees past retirement age in Chapter 7.

Pay based on the national minimum wage

The exemption covering the pay of younger workers is directly linked to the structure of the national minimum wage (NMW). It covers pay structures which use the same age bands as the NMW (meaning that employees within each age band are paid the same).

The NMW age bands are:

- aged 22 and over – the main adult rate;
- aged 22 and over – the accredited training rate (applicable in the first six months of a job with a new employer);
- 18–21 year olds – the development rate; and
- 16–17 year olds – the (lower) development rate.

The effect of the NMW exemption is as follows:

- It allows you to pay workers aged 18–21 less than you pay workers aged 22 and over, provided that you pay the 18–21-year-olds less than the main adult rate.
- It allows you to pay workers aged 18–21 more than you pay workers under 18, again provided that you pay the under eighteens less than the main adult rate.
- For pay structures which are based on age but which do not use the NMW age bands, you may be able to rely on justification (see Chapter 3), although we think that this will be extremely difficult.

Examples

An employer pays a 22-year-old £5.50 an hour (i.e. more than the NMW main adult rate of £5.35 as at 1 October 2006) and pays a 21-year-old £4.50 for doing the same job. This is lawful: the employer can rely on the NMW exemption as a defence in claims brought by the 21-year-old because they are paid less than the main adult rate.

An employer pays the NMW lower development rate (£3.00 per hour as at 1 October 2006) to workers aged 16 and 17. Once the workers reach age 18 and over, the employer pays £4.50 per hour. This is lawful: the employer can rely on the NMW exemption as a defence in claims brought by workers under 18 because they are paid less than the main adult rate.

An employer pays a 19-year-old a lower rate than it pays a 21-year-old who is doing the same job. The NMW exemption does not apply because the employer is paying a different rate of pay to workers within the same age band. In theory the employer may be able to justify this pay structure under the usual test of justification, but we think this will be extremely difficult. Therefore, this practice is likely to be unlawful.

Unfortunately, many employers pay their adult rate to 21-year-olds, not 22-year-olds as under the NMW. This means that they cannot rely on the NMW exemption if challenged by workers aged under 21 who are paid less than those in the 21 and over age group. These employers will need to change their pay structures to align them with the age bands of the NMW if they want to rely on the exemption.

If you fall into this category and plan to change your pay practice because of the age discrimination legislation, remember that this may involve changing workers' contracts or collective agreements if they provide for an adult pay rate at age 21. If you cannot reach agreement to make the change, one option is to 'red circle' the pay rate of your current workers, but raise the trigger age to 22 for new workers. We give general guidance on how to deal with potentially unlawful practices in Chapter 11, and suggest that you seek the advice of your EEF Association on how to handle a change in any particular circumstances.

Apprentices' pay

In the engineering sector it is common now for employers to award pay increases according to year of training or the apprentice achieving an NVQ or other milestone, rather than when they have a birthday. Some employers, though, still use age as their trigger for pay increases.

If you fix apprentices' pay by reference to year of training, you can probably rely on the length of service exemption (see page 72) in what we think would be the unlikely event of a claim.

You are more at risk of a claim from a young apprentice claiming equality of pay with an older apprentice if you set your apprentices' pay by reference to their age, unless you can rely on the NMW exemption. You can rely on the NMW exemption if your apprentices' pay scale mirrors the NMW age bands and/or the NMW rules on apprentices.

Apprentices who are under 19 or who have less than a year's service are not eligible for the NMW. This means you can rely on the NMW exemption to continue paying an apprentice under 19 (or one in the first year of their apprenticeship) less than an apprentice who is entitled to the NMW. It also means that you can pay two apprentices entitled to the NMW (for example, a 21- and a 23-year-old) different pay according to their age, because this ties in with the NMW age band.

If your pay scale for apprentices is based on age but you cannot rely on the NMW exemption, it is likely to be unlawful. This is because your only defence is to rely on justification (see Chapter 3), and in the circumstances we believe it would be difficult to meet the justification test. If you have such a pay scale, we suggest you consider changing to a less discriminatory one, basing pay increases on year of training or achieving other milestones, rather than age.

You may also be concerned that an apprentice may claim they should be paid the same as an older employee who is not an apprentice. Remember, to have any prospect of succeeding with a claim, the claimant has to be complaining about a difference in treatment with an appropriate comparator, i.e. someone whose circumstances are not materially different from theirs. We think that, given the special status of apprentices who, in essence, are there to be trained, they would find it very difficult to make a comparison with a non-apprentice.

Discretionary benefits based on age

You should ensure any managers who exercise discretion over awards of pay and benefits are trained to avoid making decisions which might be tainted by age discrimination.

For example, a manager might consciously or unconsciously take into account an employee's age, or base a decision on stereotypical ageist attitudes, in deciding whether to award a performance bonus or the amount of one. It is important to train managers to be aware of their obligations not to treat employees less favourably on the grounds of age (or any other prohibited ground, such as race or sex).

Benefits based on seniority

Senior employees often have more attractive benefit packages as well as higher salaries than their junior colleagues. Given that it is often older employees holding senior positions, there is a small risk that reward and remuneration practices based on seniority could be undermined by age discrimination legislation.

We think it is a small risk because employees can bring discrimination claims only by comparing their position with that of a comparable employee. If there is a material difference in job duties, skills or experience required, etc., then a claim cannot proceed. Also, it would usually be straightforward to demonstrate the business justification for rewarding senior employees more generously.

That said, we suggest you audit your practices in any event, to ensure that jobs classified as senior are, in fact, materially different from more junior positions. A risk is most likely to arise where you have two jobs that, in terms of the demands placed on employees (skill, experience, etc.), are very similar yet one of them is classified as senior, attracting more pay and benefits, and it tends to be older employees holding the senior jobs.

Pay and benefits for employees over retirement age

We deal with the issues relating to the pay and benefits of employees working beyond retirement age in Chapter 7.

11

Dealing with unlawful practices

On reading the preceding chapters on redundancy and pay and benefits, you may conclude that you are vulnerable to a legal challenge under the age discrimination legislation for a particular practice or for particular terms and conditions of the contracts with your employees. You may also consider that certain practices or terms no longer meet your business needs and that the introduction of the age discrimination legislation is a suitable moment to reconsider them.

In this chapter we consider what might be an appropriate response for you to the introduction of the legislation. In assessing how to respond to potentially unlawful practices or terms and conditions, it is important to understand the effect of a successful legal challenge against them.

Effect of a successful challenge

A successful challenge on grounds of age may result in the employment tribunal awarding financial compensation to an employee. The tribunal may also make a declaration of the employee's rights. These remedies are considered in detail in Chapter 16.

Even though the tribunal's declaration of the employee's rights and any award of compensation applies only to the individual making the claim, in practice you cannot apply the rule any longer to employees in comparable circumstances. The tribunal may also declare the rule itself void.

Your response

Our advice is that, if a claim is threatening against you and/or you believe that if one was made you might not be able to defend it, you should consider replacing the rule or policy now rather than risk having a tribunal effectively decide what the rules should be. It will be far more difficult for you to agree revised rules once a claim is made against you and even more difficult with a tribunal decision against you. Indeed, if the practice no longer meets your business needs, you may welcome the opportunity of the legislation to review it.

There are various options you can consider. You could remove the practice altogether. Clearly, this could lead to problems with employee relations as well as potential legal claims. Instead, you could tailor the practice so that you can rely on an exemption provided by the Regulations. Depending on the particular practice, this may or may not be viable. Alternatively, you could consider 'levelling up' so that all age groups are treated the same. This may not be an attractive option from the employer's perspective.

Red circling

Another option available in the case of pay and benefits is 'red circling'. You could red circle (preserve) the rights of employees who have already qualified for benefits, but change the rights for those employees who have not qualified, including new employees.

Red circling can, in certain circumstances, result in younger employees being placed at a disadvantage. We raise this issue in respect of new benefits packages for new recruits – see page 77. Because of the risk of age discrimination, before you go down the route of red circling you should consider whether you can rely on an exemption in the Regulations, and if not, whether you can meet the test of justification.

A reduction in pension benefits for new recruits may be permitted by the pensions exemption (see Chapter 14). Otherwise, you will have to justify the difference between new and old employees.

This will require you to demonstrate that you have a legitimate aim in preserving the differential. Your aim will be related to the competitive advantages of introducing the lower package of terms and the legal and employee relations problems associated with removing benefits from current employees.

Justification also requires you to demonstrate that the red circling is proportionate to that aim. In this respect, a tribunal may not consider that maintaining the red circle round pay or benefits for the duration of employment is proportionate. We therefore advise that, where possible, you aim to phase out differences in terms over time between those doing the same work, for example, by freezing pay or the value of other payments.

Flexible benefits or menu approach

As a response to potentially unlawful pay or benefits, some employers are considering offering a menu of benefits to all employees which allows them to choose their preferred benefits, up to the specified limits. This approach may help you to manage the cost of providing certain benefits to certain age groups and yet help you meet your duty not to discriminate on age grounds.

Changing contractual terms

If the practice is contractual, you will have to agree any changes with your employees. Concerns that the practice is unlawful will bolster your argument when you are seeking to negotiate changes with employees and their representatives, but unfortunately the new legislation does not give you carte blanche to override the normal rules for changing contractual terms.

To summarise, if you wish to change contractual terms, you will need the agreement of your employees or risk facing contractual or constructive dismissal claims. Agreement can be obtained either at the collective level, (through negotiation with a recognised trade union or employee representatives if that is the normal method for determining terms and conditions), or at the individual level, through the consent of each employee. For more information on changing contracts of employment, see the 'Change and reorganisation' section of the EEF Employment Guide (www.employment-guide.org.uk) or contact your EEF Association.

12

Recruitment

In this chapter we consider how common features of recruitment such as advertising and application forms are affected by the age discrimination legislation.

Age discrimination is unlawful throughout the entire recruitment process. Eliminating potentially age discriminatory language and attitudes in your recruitment practices will not only reduce the risk of an age discrimination claim, but will also help to encourage older applicants and ensure that you are recruiting from the widest pool. Remember, the age profile of the UK workforce is changing so that, increasingly, your applicants are likely to be older workers.

What the law says

The Regulations impact in the area of recruitment by making the following practices unlawful unless they can be justified:

- It is unlawful for an employer to discriminate against a person in the arrangements it makes to determine who should be offered a job. For example, this would include the selection criteria used or interview questions asked.
- It is unlawful for an employer to discriminate against a person by refusing to offer, or deliberately not offering, an applicant a job.
- It is unlawful for an employer to discriminate against a person in the terms on which it offers that person the job. For example, this means

that you must not offer inferior terms to an employee simply because they are older or younger.

- It is unlawful for an employer to discriminate against an employee in the terms on which it employs someone; for example, by offering a 66-year-old applicant a job on terms different from those offered to other permanent staff. We look at this example further at the end of this chapter.

The Regulations provide that it is *not* unlawful for an employer to discriminate at the recruitment stage (deciding to whom it should offer employment or refusing to offer employment) against job applicants:

- whose age is higher than the employer's normal retirement age (NRA – we explain this in Chapter 8) or, if there is no NRA, higher than 65;
- who will reach the NRA or age 65 within six months of making the job application.

The NRA for these purposes cannot be lower than 65.

Other than this exemption, there are no other exemptions specific to recruitment, which means that any discriminatory conduct must be justified. In a small number of circumstances, you may also be able to rely on the special defences relating to positive action or the need for a genuine occupational requirement. Since these are very unlikely to apply in practice, we do not deal with them in this Guide. An explanation of the relevant provisions is given in Appendix 1.

Justification

To justify a discriminatory recruitment practice you will need to show that the practice pursues a legitimate aim and is a proportionate means of achieving that aim (the test for justification is explained in Chapter 3).

Legitimate aims which may be relevant to recruitment include the need for a reasonable period of employment before retirement and the training requirements of the post in question.

Remember, though, that it has been established by case law that considerations of cost alone will not amount to justification. We look at some examples of justification in the context of recruitment at the end of this chapter.

Targeting particular age groups

If you are deliberately targeting candidates of a particular age group to the exclusion of others and you are challenged by an unsuccessful candidate outside the age group, you will have to justify your approach.

You may be able to justify this if you need to recruit from a particular age group in order to meet your needs in relation to succession/employment planning that you actively operate within your organisation.

For example, you have produced succession charts which have identified a lack of likely successors for particular posts when the current employees retire, which is expected to be within a few years given their age. The age of candidates will therefore be relevant to your recruitment decision to ensure an appropriate number of younger employees are available for succession. Remember, though, you will need sound evidence that the specific recruitment decision meets your particular future staffing needs. Factors such as staff turnover/retention rates will be relevant. If employees tend not to stay for more than a couple of years, you will lack the evidence to show that your practice meets your need.

Imposing any minimum age requirement for a job will also need to be justified. In practice you will be able to do this only in exceptional circumstances. Take an example of sales personnel at a luxury sports car dealership. The employer states that applicants must have a clean driving licence and also be over 25. This is because it is prohibitively expensive to obtain insurance for under-25s to drive high-performance cars. As such, their recruitment would not simply be very costly but also economically unviable for the business, unless the test driving could readily be done by another member of staff.

You may also be able to rely on the 'positive action' defence to address any imbalance in age bands within your organisation. This permits you to encourage people of a certain age group to take up employment to prevent, or compensate for, disadvantages linked to age suffered by people of that age group. For example, it would not be unlawful to state in a job advertisement that you would particularly welcome applications from older/younger workers as they are under-represented in that role within the company. You should, of course, at the same time make it clear that any appointment will be on merit alone.

It is important to note that the legislation permits 'encouragement' to apply only for a post, not positive discrimination by preferring someone because of their age. The decision as to whom to recruit must be made on merit. The positive action defence really only allows you to widen your pool of candidates.

Job specification

Recruitment should be based on competencies and experience to do the job. You should review job specification requirements and identify the relevant experience, skills and abilities that are necessary to do the job rather than insisting on a particular age qualification or number of years' experience.

The ACAS guidance suggests a three-step approach:

- Are the qualifications you require really necessary?
- Are they still current?
- Are there other ways of specifying the skill level you require?

Advertising

Ageist advertisements

As we have seen above, the Regulations make it unlawful for an employer to discriminate in relation to the arrangements it makes to determine who should be offered a job. Case law indicates that it is unlikely that placing an ageist advertisement in a newspaper will be considered as part of the 'arrangements' that an employer makes when offering employment. This means that an individual who has been discouraged from applying for a job on the basis of a discriminatory advertisement is unlikely to be able to bring an employment tribunal claim solely on that basis.

However, you still need to avoid using discriminatory language as it could be used by an unsuccessful candidate in a claim that he or she was not offered the job. For example, if an unsuccessful candidate falls outside the stated age range, he or she may assert that your decision not to recruit him or her was on grounds of age. An employment tribunal might be more easily persuaded that you did discriminate if there is evidence before the tribunal of discriminatory language used in an advertisement.

At the moment there is no statutory body to bring proceedings against an employer who places an age discriminatory advertisement. In due course, however, it is anticipated that the government's single equality commission, to be known as the Commission for Equality and Human Rights, will have that power.

Contents of advertisement

As we have highlighted above, you should be careful that any job advertisement does not contain discriminatory language. So you should avoid specifying age limits or age ranges or using words such as 'mature', 'young' or 'school leavers'. Depending on the context in which they are used, even words such as 'dynamic' or 'energetic' might suggest that young candidates will be preferred.

Asking for a particular number of years' experience is also potentially discriminatory since younger candidates may be less likely to satisfy the requirement. If, however, specific experience is necessary for the job in question, you should be able to justify the requirement unless you are asking for more experience than is really necessary to do the job. This means, however, that you should avoid automatically ruling out applications from outside the stated range.

For example, simply asking for between five and ten years' experience for, say, an HR manager may be difficult to justify if a candidate with four or fifteen years' experience would also be able to do the job. An alternative would be to state that the position would ideally suit a candidate with 5–10 years' experience.

Equally, you should consider stating that you welcome candidates from all ages and/or that candidates are considered on their merits alone in relation to the criteria for the job.

Similarly, you should not specify certain qualifications that might deter candidates of a particular age group unless these qualifications are needed for the post in question. Where appropriate, you should include the phrase 'or equivalent' when indicating relevant qualifications and make it clear that you will consider alternative equivalent qualifications.

For example, GNVQs are being phased out and being replaced by GCSEs/A levels in vocational subjects, which means that in appropriate circumstances you should state that equivalent qualifications are acceptable.

Where you place the advertisement

An individual is unlikely to be able to bring a claim solely because they were discouraged from making an application as the job was advertised in a publication which is predominantly read by a very different age group from their own.

However, you should still give some thought to where you place your advertisement as your choice of publication could be used as evidence of discriminatory intent in a claim by an unsuccessful candidate.

For example, if you advertise in a publication which has a predominantly young readership, such as the student press, an older candidate who was rejected may try to use this fact to prove that you were seeking to exclude older candidates. You would then need to explain why it was appropriate to advertise in the chosen publication and/or show that despite your choice of publication, your actions were not discriminatory, for example, because you also advertised elsewhere.

Using a recruitment agency

If you use recruitment agencies, you should be aware that you will be jointly liable if the agency discriminates whilst acting under your instruction and within its legitimate remit. Make it clear (preferably in writing) when instructing the agency that the recruitment process they undertake on your behalf should not be tainted by discrimination.

Application forms

Asking for a date of birth on your application form is not of itself age discrimination. But if you do ask for this information, you must ensure that your recruitment decision is not inappropriately influenced by age. Remember, an unsuccessful candidate may seek to argue that your decision not to recruit him or her was influenced by age. The fact that you asked for the candidate's age on the application form may mean that an employment tribunal might be more easily persuaded that you did discriminate.

You should therefore review application forms and consider removing not only date of birth, but also other unnecessary references to age such as when qualifications were obtained. In many cases, the only dates that are really necessary to help you reach a decision will be those that relate to the candidate's recent job history and experience.

Consider amending your application form to include a tear-off slip which contains the age information, which can then be used for monitoring purposes. This approach, which is recommended by ACAS, means that the information is not seen by the line manager who makes the selection but is retained by Human Resources. If you gather age information but use it only for monitoring purposes, you should make this clear on the application form and state that the age criterion will not be taken into account when making employment decisions.

Sometimes you will receive age-related information that is volunteered, for example, in a CV. But care should be taken to ensure that the candidate knows that this will not influence your employment decision. We suggest that you include an equal opportunities statement in your company documentation and make sure, of course, that it includes age diversity.

Example

> *All candidates are considered strictly on their merits in relation to the selection criteria for the job. It is our policy not to discriminate on grounds of sex, marital status, age, race, colour, nationality, ethnic or national origins, sexual orientation, disability or religious or political affiliation.*

Monitoring

As we noted in Chapter 2, many employers are already aware of the ages of their employees without having any formal monitoring system in place. However, age monitoring can also tell you whether your recruitment and selection processes are successful in recruiting a broad range of ages. You will gain a better understanding of whether your recruitment practices impact adversely on a particular age group if you monitor ages not just of the workforce but also of those shortlisted and interviewed for the job.

Selection and interviews

Assuming that the application process has been stripped of age-related references, then the selection process should simply be based on the skills and ability of the candidate. The ACAS guidance states that someone who has not been involved in the short-isting process should check that no bias, whether deliberate or unintentional, has influenced decisions, before moving on to the next stage of the recruitment process.

The important issue is to ensure that the interviewer is suitably trained about age diversity so that they know which questions should not be asked, understand that age should not affect whom they select and avoid making stereotypical assumptions.

Questions that relate to age should be avoided to prevent the candidate being under the impression that your decision will be influenced by age. Bear in mind that questions which might appear relatively innocuous could take on a different meaning in this context. Examples of questions and comments which might lead the candidate to reach that conclusion include: 'You seem to be overqualified for the job' and 'Would you feel comfortable being managed by younger staff?' The key is to keep the questioning open and non-judgemental.

All candidates should, where possible, be asked a similar set of questions to avoid a suggestion of bias, on whatever basis. Where a selection panel is used, consider whether it can be representative of different age groups.

If the candidate's age was relevant to the decision you reached, you will, of course, have to justify your decision if challenged. If so, you should ensure that you follow, and document, the process of justification (see Chapter 3) at the time you reach your decision.

Taking detailed interview notes is a practice that all HR professionals should follow as this will help demonstrate the reason why the candidate was unsuccessful and that the reason was not related to age, or if it was, that it was justified.

Graduate recruitment

Although there is no age limit for entrance to university, the vast majority of recent graduates will be in their early twenties and so graduate recruitment practices will inevitably be targeted at younger candidates. This means that you will have to justify your approach, if challenged. This may not be difficult where the job requires certain minimum levels of expertise or ability. Remember the approach that ACAS recommends and assess whether a degree qualification is required. For example, would relevant experience be sufficient? Also, consider whether it is really necessary for the candidate to be a 'recent' graduate (this is likely to depend on the actual skills needed for the job).

Ideally, you should not exclude candidates from sources other than universities. The ACAS guidance states that employers who operate 'milk round' recruitment should consider enhancing the programme with 'a broader recruitment strategy, using other avenues to capture a wider pool of applicants of differing ages'.

If you set a low maximum age in relation to your graduate recruitment and development programme, you will exclude a significant part of the talent pool – about 10 per cent of entrants on degree programmes are over 25 at the start of the programme. It will not be possible to justify doing so if it is the degree qualification alone that is necessary and not the candidate's age.

Apprentices

Apprentices are most often young. However, it is difficult to see how an employer could justify limiting its apprenticeship programmes to candidates under a certain age. Increasingly, companies are opening up their apprentice routes to older workers to meet skills shortages. For example, British Gas's 'adult traineeship scheme' had 1,200 trainees in 2003.

Of course, the main obstacle to operating a policy of recruiting apprentices of all ages is where funding is available only when the apprentice is of a particular age. For example, the Advanced Apprenticeship in Engineering Scheme attracts funding only where the apprentice is aged between 16 and 24 years.

Not taking advantage of the available funding may make the apprenticeship scheme economically unviable. In these circumstances, we think that you could justify limiting the scheme to those who qualify for funding.

The Regulations contain a special defence which applies where possessing a characteristic related to age is a 'genuine and determining occupational requirement' (GOR) (see Appendix 1). Whilst, traditionally, apprentices are school leavers who are starting out on their vocational careers, we do not think that it is a GOR to be a recent school leaver or young person to be an apprentice. In our view, this would not be a defence to imposing such a requirement on apprenticeship schemes.

Example of justification in recruitment

You have to choose between two suitably qualified candidates whose competencies are equal. One is aged 36, the other is 62. You appoint the younger candidate because you already have a number of older workers in the team who are expected to retire within the next few years and you want to recruit and train a new, younger member of staff who will be able to replace one of those employees who is expected to leave. To establish whether you can justify this approach ask yourself the following questions.

What are the potential discriminatory effects of the practice?

Rejecting the older applicant in favour of a younger candidate solely on grounds of their age, and vice versa, is age discrimination.

Why don't I want to recruit that person – what is my legitimate aim?

Analysing your workforce's age distributions as part of the preparation and implementation of succession/employment planning is generally accepted as a necessary tool in HR management. Therefore, we believe that it is capable of amounting to a legitimate aim. In this case, you are seeking to ensure that the team is not left exposed if too many employees leave within a few years of each other.

What hard evidence do I have that my approach assists in achieving that aim?
You will need to have a properly considered succession plan in operation and be able to show that you actively identify future staffing needs, develop employees to fill vacancies where appropriate, and that this recruitment decision is an informed one.

However, you will need to assess this decision against the level of staff turnover. If new employees tend not to stay for more than a couple of years, they are unlikely to be capable of being 'replacements' for those who are expected to retire in a few years' time.

Are the discriminatory effects outweighed by the objectives of the scheme?
All companies need to identify future staffing needs within their organisation and develop particular workers to fill future vacancies. As such, we believe that an effective succession planning programme will outweigh the discriminatory effects.

Could I use an alternative scheme that is less discriminatory or non-discriminatory to meet the aim?
It is difficult to see a less or a non-discriminatory alternative in this scenario where there were only two suitably trained candidates.

What do I conclude?
Your desire to recruit and train a new, younger member of staff as a replacement for one of the group of employees within the team who are expected to leave within the next few years *can* be justified in these circumstances, but only if retention rates within your organisation and/or within that role suggest that it is likely that the 36-year-old will stay in the job longer than the older candidate and/or long enough to be capable of replacing one of the older employees within the existing workforce.

13

Performance management, training and promotion

In this chapter we consider the areas of performance management, training and promotion. To avoid falling foul of the age discrimination legislation, you should ensure that your performance management system and promotion and training opportunities are based on objective assessments which should be age-neutral and do not include any unnecessary age barriers.

What the law says

The Regulations make it unlawful for an employer to discriminate against a worker on grounds of age 'in the opportunities it affords him or her for promotion, a transfer or training', unless it can justify its actions.

You could therefore act unlawfully if, for example, you limit your workers' opportunities for promotion or development on grounds of their age and you cannot justify doing so, or if your approach to performance management is influenced by stereotypical assumptions about the ages of your workers. We examine these issues below.

For consideration of the justification test, see Chapter 3.

Performance management and promotion

An area you will need to consider in light of age discrimination legislation is your approach to performance management and promotion of workers, young and old. For example, are younger, or older, workers excluded from consideration for promotion? Is promotion based on length of service? Is a different attitude taken to performance of older rather than younger workers?

Appraisals

Good performance management will improve the effectiveness and individual development of a worker and should also improve the performance of the business. It is an essential tool in monitoring workforce performance, good and bad. Monitoring employees' performance should be a consistent and objective process at all stages of their careers, regardless of their age. Equally, tackling poor performance, again whatever the employee's age, also needs to be underpinned by an effective performance management system.

If older employees' performance tends not to be as closely managed as that of younger employees within your organisation, then you should take steps to address this. Allowing older workers to 'cruise towards retirement' is really no longer an option because in the coming years more and more employees may wish to work for longer and exercise their right to request not to retire. You may have already decided to remove your retirement age, thereby making effective performance management more important than ever.

Not managing older employees effectively is, of course, treating them more favourably than younger employees, who would then have cause for complaint. Appendix 2 contains details on managing and motivating your older workforce.

Training of those giving appraisals

Line managers and everyone involved in the appraisal process must be properly trained to challenge assumptions and to look at the actual performance of individuals.

Equally, care should be taken to avoid the use of discriminatory language in the appraisal process, such as 'given his age he is still giving a solid performance' or 'for one so young she shows impressive communication skills'.

This is particularly important where an individual's performance is ranked relative to their peers. Not only is discriminatory language irrelevant to the assessment of performance, it could also be used as evidence of discriminatory intent in a claim by an employee who is dissatisfied with their appraisal. An employment tribunal might be more easily persuaded that discrimination has occurred if there is evidence before the tribunal of discriminatory language used in the appraisal process.

For example, an employee who received a smaller pay rise or bonus than colleagues on the basis of a poor appraisal which contained discriminatory language will be able to show facts which, if they went unchallenged, may be sufficient to enable the tribunal to conclude that there has been discrimination. You would then need to explain why it was appropriate to award the pay rise or bonus that you did and that your actions were not discriminatory.

Promotion

Every company needs to identify future staffing needs within their organisation and develop particular workers to fill future vacancies. This means that employers should monitor career progression amongst all groups, whatever their age. Workers should have a clear understanding of how their work and performance in their role affect the performance of the business as a whole.

If your decision about an employee's promotion is influenced by their age, you will need to justify your decision. We believe that this will be difficult because promotion opportunities should not be influenced by age but simply by the skills to do the job. However, the ACAS guidance does state that you may be able to justify fixing a maximum age for promotion of employees and the maximum age might reflect the training requirements of the post or the need for a reasonable period of employment before retirement.

With more employees working beyond 65 it may be that junior members of the workforce see fewer opportunities for their own promotion and development. This could lead to retention problems and you may need to adopt initiatives to address this, such as introducing an attractive benefits package, keeping pay in line with the market rate, focusing on career paths and personal development, or employees' work/life balance. Remember also that it is important to manage the performance of all workers effectively, regardless of their age.

Training

You should ensure that relevant training options and programmes are available to all your employees and that there are no age-related barriers which would prevent equal access. Your training strategy should not only meet your business needs, but also identify individual development goals.

Many employers, notably those with IiP (Investors in People) accreditation, will have in place a programme which identifies training needs within the workforce. But when assessing the training needs of your workforce you may need to challenge some stereotypical assumptions – for example, that older workers are not interested in learning new skills or are uncomfortable with Information Technology.

There are, of course, a variety of training methods available and many employers adopt a flexible training programme in terms of both content and method of training delivery, taking account of personal learning preferences. Offering a diverse training programme is likely to benefit a greater number of employees.

Some employers are reluctant to invest training resources in older workers as they think that these employees are heading towards retirement at 65. Not offering such workers training is unlawful age discrimination unless you can justify your approach. Justification will be difficult unless the training in question is lengthy and you will not see the benefit of that training over a reasonable time period before retirement.

As we explain in Chapter 3, to justify a discriminatory practice you will need to show that the practice pursues a legitimate aim and is a proportionate means of achieving that aim. Take the example of where you offer financial assistance for certain employees to undertake a Master of Business Administration degree. You may be able to justify limiting such funding to younger employees who are a long way off retirement because your aim is to ensure, as far as possible, that the business gains the benefit of the skills they learn over a significant period in the future. Taking into account the length of time required to complete an MBA, applying an age limit may be a proportionate means of achieving this aim.

However, do not forget that if staff turnover in your organisation is high, it will be difficult to argue that it is a reasonable business decision not to offer the training when in any event employees do not stay with the company more than a few years. (Of course, some employees will request to work beyond 65 and, if so, you may see the benefits of training beyond the retirement age if you grant that request.)

It may be necessary to provide specific training to help managers manage a more age-diverse workforce. Appendix 2 contains further details.

Apprentices

It is difficult to see how an employer could justify limiting apprenticeship programmes to candidates under a certain age. Increasingly, companies are opening up their apprentice routes to older workers to meet skills shortages. There is, however, one circumstance that could justify limiting apprenticeships to younger workers and this is where the apprenticeship programme is a funded scheme and where funding is available only when the apprentice is of a particular age (see also Chapter 12).

Work experience

It is also unlawful to discriminate against those to whom you offer or provide practical work experience. For example, although work experience is usually undertaken by recent school leavers we do not believe that you could justify refusing, on grounds of age, an application from an older person for work experience.

The age discrimination legislation also extends to the providers of vocational training (which is beyond the scope of this Guide).

Positive action

The legislation permits you to encourage people of a certain age group to take up training opportunities to help fit them for particular work to prevent, or compensate for, disadvantages linked to age suffered by those people in that age group. This is the special defence of positive action. For example, you may be seeking to encourage people of a particular age group to apply for certain training opportunities because there are very few or no other employees within that age group within your organisation with those skills.

Although positive action can help you address any age imbalance within your workforce, it is important to note that it is only 'encouragement' to apply for training, not positive discrimination by preferring someone because of their age, that is permissible.

Monitoring

We recommend that you monitor which employees apply for, are offered and undertake training and promotion. This should reveal whether there is disparity in training undertaken/promotions awarded between the age groups and whether you need to take steps to address the imbalance.

14

Pensions

The age legislation contains special pension exemptions which cover many long-standing and common practices in the operation of occupational pension schemes, in particular the central features of a defined benefit scheme. However, the exemptions are narrowly drafted so it is important that you ask your pensions advisers to check that your practices are in fact covered. In particular, it is likely that you will have to change the way you treat employees who stay on after retirement age, or risk age discrimination complaints.

Overview

The general rule under the age discrimination legislation is that employers, trustees and managers are not permitted to discriminate on grounds of age in relation to pension benefits or the administration of the pension scheme, (except in relation to rights accrued or benefits payable for periods of service before 1 October 2006).

Most pension arrangements are designed around age or age-related rules. However, the legislation contains special pension exemptions which provide that specified pension arrangements remain lawful even though they amount to age discrimination. The protected arrangements are listed under 'Detail of the pension exemptions' below. Overall, the impact of the pensions exemptions is as follows.

Age and seniority

Generally speaking, the practical effect of the pension exemptions is to allow employers operating occupational pension schemes (as opposed to group personal pension schemes, see 'Personal pensions' below) to:

- apply different rules within a single pension scheme for determining the minimum or maximum age for admission for different groups of employees; and/or
- different rules between pension schemes for the same purpose.

Also, you can continue to use age in actuarial calculations to determine the amount of benefit and levels of employer and employee contribution, without risk of a legal challenge under the legislation.

You can also vary the employer and/or employee contributions according to the level of pensionable pay. This means that, as level of pensionable pay is broadly related to seniority, you can continue to make such distinctions based on seniority (although some schemes may have to consider whether to change their definitions, to refer to salary levels rather than job titles, in order to fit the relevant exemption more closely).

Whilst the exemptions cover the practice of setting a maximum age for admission to a particular scheme and a maximum number of years for accruing benefit, they do not cover a rule that sets a maximum age for accruing benefits (most commonly, the retirement age). If you stop employees who work on beyond retirement from continuing to accrue benefits under your pension scheme, they will have a claim for age discrimination unless you can justify the practice, which may be difficult.

You should, therefore, check with your pension scheme adviser what the scheme rules are in relation to employees staying in employment beyond retirement age. It may be that you have none, because historically employees have not stayed on after retirement age. On the other hand, you may have rules that are now potentially unlawful, unless you can justify them. Now is the time to review them to ensure that they are lawful and fit with your remuneration and reward strategy, given that employees may make requests to continue working after retirement age.

Length of service

There is a specific pension exemption which provides that you can continue to use length of service:

- as part of the calculation for determining benefits within a group of comparable employees - for example, a calculation of 15/60ths for an employee with 15 years' pensionable service; and/or
- to set a minimum period of service (of not more than two years) for eligibility to receive benefits from the scheme.

Without the exemption, those employers for whom there is a broad association in their workforce between length of service and age would have had to justify any difference in the amount of pension benefit received by employees with differing lengths of service, if challenged.

However, the pension exemption dealing with length of service does not cover using length of service over two years more generally to set, for example, eligibility for joining a scheme, or the level of contributions or type of benefit structure. There is, though, another specific pension exemption that covers a decision to close a scheme (or a section of the scheme) to new members (see 'Detail of the pension exemptions' below).

For example, suppose, in December 2000, in response to your pension scheme deficit, you introduced a new section of your defined benefit (DB) scheme for employees joining you after 1 January 2001. The new DB section had a lower accrual rate (1/80th, instead of 1/60th) and you required employees to make higher contributions than those in the other section of the scheme. They may also have a higher pension age. Alternatively, you may have established a defined contribution (DC) scheme for them. All of these common practices are permitted by different aspects of the pension exemptions.

In contrast, if you only allow employees with more than ten years' service, irrespective of their start date, to join your DB scheme, the length of service pension exemption would not apply. If a young employee with seven years' service doing the same job as a longer-serving older colleague is aggrieved that their pension benefits are inferior and makes a claim, you cannot rely on the pension exemption, but you may be able to rely on the length of service exemption for pay and benefits (see Chapter 10).

Remember that the pension exemptions cover pension arrangements only; they do not cover retirement ages. So, you cannot rely on the pension exemptions to operate different retirement ages for employees doing the same job, but you can rely on it to operate different pensionable ages.

Detail of the pension exemptions

If you operate an occupational pension scheme (as distinct from a group personal pension scheme; see below), the pension exemptions permit you to continue, without risk of legal challenge, practices that involve using certain age or age-related factors to determine, for example, the level of contributions you make into your pension scheme.

In reading the paragraphs below remember there is a distinction between the age at which you may require employees to retire ('the retirement age'), and the age at which they can draw their full pension without actuarial reduction, namely, pensionable age. The two may be the same because of the obvious linkage between them, but they do not have to be.

In many schemes, pensionable age is not a single age but an age range; employees who retire within the age range take their benefit without actuarial reduction, but those who retire after it are paid actuarially enhanced benefits. Under the Regulations, the beginning and end of this range are defined respectively as the 'early retirement pivot age', the earliest age at which a member can retire and be paid benefits without actuarial reduction, and the 'late retirement pivot age', the age from which an employee's benefits are actuarially enhanced because they retired 'late'. The practices covered by the pension exemptions are detailed below:

Closing pension schemes

The regulations provide exemptions for:

- Closing pension schemes or sections of them to new members (which would otherwise be discriminatory if new recruits tend to be younger). If you wish to rely on this exemption, the scheme must be closed to employees who are already employed by you but who have not yet joined the scheme, as well as to new recruits.

Age

The regulations provide exemptions for:

- Using age criteria in actuarial calculations for determining, for example, employer or employee contributions, for calculating the amount a benefit should be enhanced or reduced for either late or early payment, or for fixing the amount of a lump sum on retirement.
- In most schemes, setting a maximum or minimum age for admission, including different ages for different groups or categories of employees.
- Setting a normal pension age in a scheme (i.e. an age at which employees normally become entitled to receive retirement benefits without actuarial reduction or enhancement) or an early or late retirement pivot age, including different ages for different groups or categories of employee.
- In DB schemes, using age to set different levels of employee or employer contributions amongst those whose benefits are calculated on the same fraction of pensionable pay (to take account of the fact that it costs you more to provide the benefit as members get older).
- Similarly, under DC schemes, setting different levels of employer or employee contributions according to the age of the employee if your objective is to equalise or broadly equalise the benefits employees receive on retirement irrespective of their age whilst in service with you. Conversely, you can maintain equal contribution rates even if it means employees receive different benefits on retirement because of their ages whilst in pensionable service with you.

Length of service

The regulations provide exemptions for:

- Capping the number of years of pensionable service that can be counted when calculating benefit.
- In DB schemes, using length of pensionable service to determine the amount of a final salary pension (for example, 15/60ths or 15/80ths), so long as the same fraction of pensionable pay for each year of pensionable service is used for comparable employees. This exemption means that a central feature of DB schemes, which would otherwise be discriminatory if shorter-serving employees tend to be younger, is excluded from challenge under the age legislation.
- Setting a minimum period of employment before employees can receive benefits as long as the period is not more than two years.

Pay (including seniority)

The regulations provide exemptions for:

- Taking pensionable pay into account in calculating pension benefits (which could disadvantage younger employees if higher-paid employees tend to be older in your company).
- Capping the amount of pensionable pay that can be taken into account in calculating the benefit payable (which might disadvantage older, higher-paid employees if there is a broad association between age and pay in your company).
- Setting different levels of employer and/or employee contributions depending on level of pensionable pay.
- Setting a minimum level of pensionable pay for employees to receive benefits as long as the minimum level of pay is not above the lower earnings limit for National Insurance contributions.

Miscellaneous

The regulations provide exemptions for:

- Paying bridging pensions for male employees, paid between 60 and 65, to compensate them for the fact they are not entitled to the basic state pension whereas women over 60 are.
- Fixing a maximum age for transfers in or out of a scheme as long as it is not more than one year before the scheme's normal pension age.
- Enhancing an early retirement pension for an employee retiring before the early retirement pivot age on ill-health grounds by crediting them with years of pensionable service lost. This prevents older ill-health retirees claiming they have been credited with fewer years' service than younger ones.
- Reducing the amount of pension paid to a member's dependant who is more than a specified number of years younger than the pension scheme member.
- Stopping life assurance for members who have retired on ill-health grounds once they reach 65 (or the retirement age, if different).
- Increasing pensions in payment only for members over the age of 55, or by different rates according to the age of the pensioner (if your aim is to maintain the value of the pensions of older members compared with younger ones), or by the length of time the pension has been in payment (again, where your aim is to maintain the relative value of members' pensions).

Enhanced retirement benefits on redundancy

Some occupational pension schemes allow employees over a certain age to retire early, particularly in a redundancy situation, either without actuarial reduction or with an enhancement to their years of pensionable service.

If, for example, the cut-off age is 55, an employee made redundant under age 55 and so not eligible for the early retirement benefit may be aggrieved by this difference in treatment, which is directly related to their age.

The pension exemption applies to rules in a DB scheme that permits employees to retire before the scheme's early retirement pivot age (which might, for example, be 60) once they have reached a minimum age (commonly 55), but only if the pension benefit is actuarially reduced and the employee is not credited with additional periods of pensionable service.

However, there is a further exemption for employees who were active or prospective members of your DB scheme on 1 October 2006. In their case only, it is permissible for an early retirement pension to be paid without actuarial reduction or for the employee to be credited with extra pensionable service.

If you do not change your scheme rules for employees whom you recruit after 1 October 2006, an employee aged 53, for example, who is not eligible for payment of early retirement benefits without actuarial reduction or with enhanced pensionable service could bring a discrimination claim citing as a comparator a 55-year-old recruited after 1 October 2006. Your eligibility rule would be unlawful on age grounds unless you can justify the practice if challenged, which we think is unlikely (see Chapter 9).

Personal pensions

There is an exemption that applies to group personal pension schemes, (established by employers via a contract with a commercial provider). The exemption is more limited than those set out above for occupational pension schemes.

The exemption covers your use of age criteria in setting employer or employee contribution rates. You can continue, without risk of legal challenge, to set different levels of contributions based on age as long as you are doing so to equalise, or broadly equalise, the benefits employees receive on retirement irrespective of their age whilst in pensionable service with you (given that it costs more to provide the pension benefits for an older member than a younger one). Unless that is your aim, you cannot rely on the exemption to use age to set different levels of contribution, including for those continuing to work for you after 65. Instead, you would have to justify any differences in treatment in the normal way (see Chapter 3).

The exemption also covers a policy of making different levels of employer contribution according to salary level. As long as your rules for making contributions refer to salary levels rather than grade, you can continue to differentiate between employees according to seniority without having to justify the practice.

If you make different levels of employer contributions according to length of service, you cannot rely on this exemption. For example, if you pay contributions towards the personal pensions of only those employees with more than 5 years' service (and there is a broad association between age and length of service in your workforce) to encourage loyalty or motivation or to reward experience, you may be able to rely on the long service exemption for pay and benefits if challenged (see Chapter 10 for details).

Practices outside the exemptions

The pension exemption covers many of the common, long-standing pension practices in occupational pension schemes, especially those operated by private sector companies.

That said, it is possible that your scheme contains a rule or practice that is not on the list of protected practices. Alternatively, your scheme may not qualify for a particular exemption because it does not meet the technical definitions in the legislation. In these cases, your practice or rule is potentially unlawful on grounds of age discrimination if you cannot justify it or cannot rely on the length of service exemption for pay and benefits as an alternative (see Chapter 10).

Therefore, you should ask your pension scheme advisers to audit your pension arrangements to identify any potentially unlawful practices and consider changing them. Bear in mind that you do not have carte blanche to make changes. You will have to take advice on the appropriate procedure for making amendments to your pension arrangements. Contact your EEF Association for further advice on the employment law implications and your usual pension advisers.

Government guidance

DTI guidance on the effect of the legislation on pension arrangements is available at www.dti.gov.uk/er/equality/age.htm.

15

Harassment

In this chapter, we consider the types of behaviour that could result in a claim of harassment on the grounds of age, and what employers can do to minimise their risk of liability.

The Regulations outlaw harassment at work on the grounds of age, either by co-workers or by management.

Who is protected?

As for most of the age discrimination legislation, it is not just employees and job applicants who are protected against harassment. Anyone who enters into a contract to do work personally for an employer is also protected, such as self-employed contractors and workers who are supplied to do work by a third party.

What counts as harassment?

The definition of harassment is the same as that in the sex, race and disability discrimination legislation:

> An individual is harassed where, on the grounds of age (their own or another's), that individual is subjected to unwanted conduct which has the purpose or effect of violating his or her dignity or creating an intimidating, hostile, degrading, humiliating or offensive environment for him or her.
>
> Whether conduct has the effects above is a question that should be assessed objectively, having regard to all the circumstances, in particular the individual who makes the complaint.

Harassment can occur even where the perpetrator does not intend to cause offence.

Preventing ageist harassment may involve a cultural shift in your workplace. Remarks, banter and jokes about age may be commonplace and considered acceptable. They may not always be recognised as potentially offensive.

We set out below some examples of behaviour that, *depending on the circumstances*, could potentially amount to harassment on the grounds of age:

- Ageist jokes whether made verbally, in birthday cards or in emails.
- Using ageist labels that individuals may find demeaning, such as 'young man' or 'girl' or 'grandpa'.
- Derogatory comments related to someone's age or perceived age-related characteristics, such as someone being 'wet behind the ears', 'unable to learn new tricks', 'over the hill' or 'past his prime'.
- The social exclusion of older or younger colleagues.
- Bullying behaviour which is connected to age.

Context of the behaviour

Whether or not particular behaviour falls within the definition of harassment will depend on the context. So, whilst isolated instances of less serious types of behaviour are unlikely to amount to harassment, the same behaviour could be categorised as harassment if it took place alongside other ill-treatment or formed part of a continued campaign of harassment or bullying.

For example, an ageist joke directed at a team member by a manager in a team meeting, during which that person's performance had been publicly derided, will clearly be more serious than if the same joke were made during some birthday drinks in a more sociable setting.

Who can be liable for harassment?

Both the employer and the perpetrator of the harassment can be liable for the harassment of an individual.

As an employer, you will be liable for harassment committed at work by someone employed by you. You can even be liable for harassment which occurs at a social event outside the workplace, if the event can properly be described as an extension of employment, for instance a leaving party organised and paid for by the company.

You can be liable for the acts of employees, apprentices and anyone that has entered into a contract with you to provide work personally, such as a self-employed contractor or agency worker. However, you will not be liable if one of your workers is harassed by someone outside of these categories, such as a supplier or customer.

If harassment takes place during the course of employment, you can be liable even though you did not know about or approve of the behaviour.

Avoiding liability

You can avoid liability for acts of harassment by your workers if you can prove that you took all reasonably practicable steps to prevent them doing the act in question whilst at work. You will not be able to rely on this defence if you failed to do this, even if taking those steps would not have prevented the particular discrimination occurring.

Example

An employee is bullied by his manager. Sometimes the bullying includes an element of harassment on the grounds of his age. The company dignity at work policy prohibits bullying, but it has not been updated to include any reference to harassment on the grounds of age.

Implementing a policy which makes it clear that harassment on the grounds of age is unacceptable is a reasonably practicable step for an employer to take to prevent such harassment. Since it has failed to do this, the employer cannot avoid liability for the manager's actions. This is the case even though it is unlikely that an updated policy would have stopped the harassment, since it did not stop the bullying.

Preventing harassment

In order to establish that you have taken all steps that are reasonable to prevent your workers from harassing colleagues and therefore to avoid liability for any such acts, you need to take the following steps.

Put in place a comprehensive policy against such behaviour

This should make clear what type of conduct will be viewed as harassment and that it will not be tolerated. It should also set out an accessible and clear procedure for individuals to follow if they wish to complain informally or formally about harassment. Such a procedure should comply with the statutory dispute resolution rules (see the EEF publication, *Dispute Resolution: A Practical Guide to the New Law*).

The easiest way to introduce such a policy is to update any existing harassment or dignity at work policy. A model policy is available at www.employmentguide.org.uk.

Communicate the policy to all those who work for you

Preferably, this should be done by giving all workers, including self-employed contractors, temporary employees, seconded and agency workers, an electronic or paper copy of the policy and explaining the content to them. Ideally, they should be asked to acknowledge in writing that they have received a copy and understand its contents. For new workers this should take place during the induction process.

Train all workers on how to avoid harassment

Initially the concept of age discrimination will be new to many workers. We therefore recommend that training includes plenty of examples of what might constitute harassment relating to age. It might be useful to provide a note reminding workers of what was discussed at the training.

This should be combined with an explanation of the new policy.

Managers, supervisors and employee representatives should be given specific training on how to prevent and deal with harassment on the grounds of age and on how to operate the relevant policy (see also the next step).

Records should be kept of the nature of the training and who has received it.

Ensure that managers intervene

Ensure that managers are proactive in intervening if they become aware of any activities amongst their teams that could amount to harassment, even where they have received no complaints. This could amount to little more than pointing out to individuals the effect their behaviour might have on others and asking them to stop.

Intervention will help to prevent situations arising where workers feel that they have been harassed and may influence attitudes in the workplace about the acceptability of ageist comments, jokes and stereotyping.

Deal properly with complaints

If an individual complains formally or informally about harassment on the grounds of age, as with any other type of harassment complaint, management should take the complaint seriously and deal with it appropriately and promptly in accordance with their policy. If the grievance is in writing, then the statutory grievance procedures should be followed (see the EEF publication *Dispute Resolution: A Practical Guide to the New Law*).

Remedies for harassment

An individual who alleges harassment on the grounds of age has several possible claims against his or her employer, as follows:

- Harassment in contravention of the Regulations. The remedies for this are described in Chapter 16.
- Unfair constructive dismissal where the employee believes he or she had grounds to resign on the basis that the employer, by not

tackling the harassment effectively, had broken its implied contractual obligation to maintain a relationship of trust and confidence.

- Harassment under the Protection from Harassment Act 1997, where the harasser pursued a course of conduct during the course of employment which he or she knew, or ought to have known, amounted to harassment.
- Compensation for negligence if he or she was so badly harassed that he or she suffers a foreseeable physical or psychiatric illness or injury as a result

A claim of harassment on the grounds of age may also be accompanied by other discrimination claims, whether on the basis of age or otherwise.

For example, an employee might claim that harassment was related to both age and sex and could bring complaints under the age and sex discrimination legislation. Alternatively, an employee who claims that he was harassed on the grounds of age by his manager might also claim that his manager's failure to promote him amounted to age discrimination.

The statutory grievance procedures will apply to claims of harassment on the grounds of age and constructive dismissal. As a consequence, an individual may normally present a complaint of constructive dismissal or harassment on the grounds of age to the employment tribunal only if he or she has raised the grievance in writing with the employer and waited 28 days. For more information on the operation of the statutory grievance procedures and time limits in discrimination claims, see the EEF publication *Dispute Resolution, A Practical Guide to the New Law.*

16

Remedies

In this chapter, we:

- explore the remedies available to a claimant who successfully brings proceedings under the Regulations;
- focus in detail on compensation, and how employment tribunals are likely to approach this issue;
- detail the time limits within which a claimant must bring proceedings under the age discrimination legislation; and
- deal briefly with the impact of the statutory grievance procedure.

Remedies for unlawful age discrimination

Where an employment tribunal finds that a claimant has been discriminated against or harassed on grounds of age, it can:

- order the employer to pay the claimant compensation;
- make an order declaring the employee's/employer's rights; and/or
- recommend that the employer takes action within a specific time-frame to remove or mitigate the adverse effect of the discrimination on the individual claimant.

All of these remedies are common to other forms of unlawful discrimination, for example sex and race discrimination.

Compensation

It is important for two reasons that you as the employer understand how much a claim might be worth. First, if you are in receipt of a claim, you need to establish its potential value to help you decide whether to defend it or settle it. Second, having an understanding as to how compensation is calculated under the Regulations will assist you when undertaking the risk assessment we advocate at Chapter 2.

There are two key factors you should bear in mind when looking at compensation for unlawful age discrimination. First, such awards are uncapped; and second, an employment tribunal can make an award to reflect the claimant's injury to feelings. These two factors mean that age discrimination claims can be extremely costly.

Calculating compensation

Compensation is calculated in the same way for all of the existing discrimination laws. Essentially, the aim is that the claimant must, as far as possible, be put into the position he or she would have been in had the discrimination not occurred.

By way of illustration, if an employee successfully argues that he was not recruited on grounds of his age, a tribunal will take into account the following factors in assessing compensation: the individual's chances of being offered the job if the discrimination had not taken place; the salary and benefits he would have received had he been recruited to the role; the length of time he would have been likely to remain in that job; and the length of time it would take him to find other employment, on the assumption he took reasonable steps to do so.

Of course, sometimes claimants will bring an age discrimination claim alongside other claims such as unfair dismissal, sex discrimination or disability discrimination. If you are faced with this situation, bear in mind that claimants will not be compensated twice in respect of the same loss.

Note that the tribunal can award compensation for unintentional indirect discrimination on grounds of age only if it has made either a declaration or recommendation (see below) and it considers it just and equitable to award compensation as well.

Injury to feelings

The Regulations provide that tribunals may award compensation for injury to feelings caused by the discriminatory conduct, even if no other compensation is awarded.

In 2003, the Court of Appeal gave judgment in a sex discrimination case that established that compensation for injury to feelings falls into three bands. Employment tribunals will follow this guidance in making awards under the age discrimination legislation. The three bands are set out below, though it is likely that inflation will be factored in:

- A top band of £15,000–25,000 in the most serious cases, such as where there has been a lengthy campaign of discriminatory harassment. This should be exceeded in only the most exceptional cases.
- A middle band of £5,000–15,000 for serious cases which do not merit an award in the top band.
- Awards of £500–5,000 for less serious cases, such as where the act of discrimination is an isolated or one-off occurrence. Generally, tribunals will avoid awards of less than £500.

Declaration of employee's rights

An employment tribunal can also issue an order declaring the employee's rights. Essentially, this is simply a statement that the employer has violated the employee's rights and is appropriate where the claimant has suffered no loss and the tribunal makes no award for injury to feelings.

Recommendation that the employer takes action

An employment tribunal may recommend steps to be taken within a specified period so as to lessen or reduce the adverse effect of the discrimination on the individual claimant. Case law under the sex discrimination legislation states that an employment tribunal cannot make a recommendation that a discriminatory practice should cease altogether.

An example of a recommendation made under existing sex discrimination law is that a worker who had been sexually harassing a claimant be moved to a post elsewhere within the employer's organisation.

Failure to comply with a recommendation in a case where the employment tribunal has already awarded compensation can lead to a further increase in the compensation awarded. It can also lead to an order for compensation being made where one had not previously been made.

Remedies for unfair dismissal

The Regulations also make important changes to the unfair dismissal regime contained within the Employment Rights Act 1996. First, the upper age limit to claim unfair dismissal has been removed. This means that the right to claim unfair dismissal is conferred, for the first time, on those aged 65 and over. Second, retirement becomes a potentially fair reason for dismissal. Even so, in certain circumstances, employees who are compulsorily retired may be able to claim unfair dismissal (see Chapter 8).

Where an employment tribunal finds that a claimant has been unfairly dismissed, it can:

- order the employer to pay the claimant compensation; and/or
- make an order for reinstatement or re-engagement.

Compensation

Unfair dismissal awards comprise two elements: the basic and compensatory award.

Basic award

The basic award is calculated according to a standard formula which is easy to calculate and predict, and is in fact calculated in the same way as a statutory redundancy payment (see Chapter 9).

However, where an employment tribunal finds that the reason, or the primary reason, for dismissal is retirement, but the dismissal is unfair because the employer has failed to follow the required procedural steps, an employment tribunal must make a minimum basic award of four weeks' pay, unless it considers that such an award would result in injustice to the employer. For these purposes a week's pay is capped (at the time of writing, at £290). This provision will be relevant where the employer has failed in any or all of the following duties: 1) giving fall-back notification; 2) considering the employee's request not to retire; or 3) considering the employee's appeal, if any, against a decision not to grant the employee's request.

Compensatory award

Compensatory awards are awarded according to what the employment tribunal '*considers just and equitable in all the circumstances, having regard to the loss sustained by the complainant in consequence of the dismissal in so far as that loss is attributable to action taken by the employer*'. They are, however, subject to an overall cap, which at the time of writing stands at £58,400.

Removal of the upper age limit

A key question raised by the removal of the upper age limit of 65 for claiming unfair dismissal is how employment tribunals are going to approach calculating the compensatory award for unfair dismissal.

Until October 2006, tribunals tended to use the company's normal retirement age, or age 65, as a cut-off point when assessing an employee's future losses.

Following the removal of the upper age limit, however, employees are likely to argue that they should be awarded losses past 65 or the NRA if it is common for their employer to allow employees to work on past those ages. An employee is unlikely to succeed in this argument where an employer maintains a retirement age of 65 and allows individuals to stay on in exceptional circumstances only. Where an employer has a flexible policy on retirement and in fact allows most employees to stay on past 65, however, it increases the risk of an employee successfully claiming future losses post-65. In practice, employment tribunals will be largely influenced by an employer's policies and practices on retirement.

Retirement dismissals which are unfair because of failure to follow the procedure for considering a request

In certain situations, dismissal by reason of compulsory retirement will be unfair only by virtue of failing to follow the procedure for considering a request (see Chapter 8).

In such a case, you could argue that the compensatory award should be limited to the length of time it would have taken you to follow the procedure properly, as you would still have dismissed the employee in any event. Employment tribunals might accept this argument. Alternatively, employment tribunals might make an award on the basis of the chances of the employee staying on had the procedure been followed.

Reinstatement and re-engagement

Where there has been an unfair dismissal, the employment tribunal can order reinstatement or re-engagement if the claimant so wishes. Reinstatement is an order that the employee be reinstated in his or her job with no financial loss. Re-engagement is an order that the employee must be re-engaged in a job comparable to that from which he or she was dismissed, or in other suitable employment.

In practice, re-employment orders are very rare. According to the Employment Tribunals Service Annual Report 2004/2005, such orders were made in only 0.2 per cent of unfair dismissal cases which proceeded to hearing between 1 April 2004 and 31 March 2005.

The interaction of age discrimination and unfair dismissal claims

Where they are entitled to do so, claimants are likely to plead both age discrimination *and* unfair dismissal. In practice, if they are successful in both claims, an employment tribunal will award compensation under the age discrimination legislation because it is uncapped, and there is scope for awards for injury to feelings.

Example

B, aged 60, is dismissed because he is told he is 'too old' and no longer fits in with the otherwise young team. He can bring both an unlawful age discrimination claim and an unfair dismissal claim against his employer. If he is successful in both claims, he can claim a basic award and, if he so wishes, seek reinstatement or re-engagement under the unfair dismissal law. However, it is in B's interests to obtain compensation under the age discrimination legislation so that the upper limit on the compensatory award will not bite. B can then also claim injury to feelings.

However, claimants whose claim relates to compulsory retirement at age 65 or above can rely only on an unfair dismissal rather than an age discrimination claim.

Example

F is compulsorily retired on his 66th birthday. His employer has a company-wide NRA of 70. F cannot bring an unlawful age discrimination claim because the Regulations stipulate that it is not unlawfully discriminatory to retire an employee at or above age 65. He can, however, claim unfair dismissal because his employer is retiring him before the NRA (see Chapter 8). In these circumstances, the maximum value of F's claim is (at the time of writing) £58,400, the maximum compensatory award set down by legislation, plus the maximum basic award available, which (at the time of writing) is £8,700.

Stand-alone remedy of up to eight weeks' pay

Where a tribunal finds that an employer has failed to give standard notification (i.e. to notify the employee in writing, 6–12 months prior to the intended date of retirement (IDR), of the IDR and of the employee's right to request not to retire), it can award up to eight weeks' pay to the employee. A week's pay for these purposes is subject to a cap set down in the legislation. At the time of writing this stands at £290 and so the most an employee could be awarded for breach of this duty is currently £2,320.

Employment tribunals must make this award on a just and equitable basis. In our view, there is therefore scope to argue before a tribunal that an award should be much less that the full eight weeks, perhaps even a nil award.

Example

An employer does not give standard notification to an employee, B. It does, however, provide B with fall-back notification and gives her this information in writing five months prior to her IDR. As a consequence, B puts in a request to carry on working past retirement, which is accepted. There must be room to argue that it would not be just and equitable for B to receive any compensation in respect of the employer's failure to give her standard notification, because it has had no practical impact on her. The employer has still considered, and granted, B's request, so any additional money would simply represent a windfall for her.

Denial of the right to be accompanied

An employee has a right to be accompanied by a companion to a meeting held under the procedure for considering a request (see Chapter 6).

Where an employment tribunal finds that an employer has failed, or threatened to fail, to comply with this right, it can order the employer to pay the employee up to two weeks' pay. A week's pay for these purposes is again subject to the maximum amount set down in the legislation, which at the time of writing is £290.

In addition to this, if the tribunal finds that the employer treated the employee less favourably because he exercised (or sought to exercise) his right to be accompanied, then it can make a declaration to that effect and make an award of compensation to the employee. Similarly, the tribunal can make a declaration and an award of compensation in respect of a worker who was treated less favourably by the employer because he accompanied (or sought to accompany) an employee to a meeting held under the procedure.

Other rights

A party interested in a contract can apply to the court for a void or unenforceable term to be removed or modified.

A person can also present a complaint to an employment tribunal that a term or rule of a collective agreement is void if he or she believes that the term or rule may at some future time affect him or her. If the employment tribunal finds the complaint to be well founded, it can make an order declaring the offending term or rule void.

Appendix 1

What the law says

The provisions of the Regulations are described in detail here.

What the law says

1. The Regulations apply –

- to employment at an establishment in Great Britain (GB). This is (i) where the work is done wholly or partly in GB or (ii) if done wholly outside GB, where the employer has a place of business in GB, the work is for the purposes of the business carried on there and the worker is ordinarily resident in GB either at the time of applying for or getting the job or at any time during the employment. The Northern Ireland Regulations have the same provision referring to employment at an establishment in Northern Ireland.
- to employees under a contract of employment; to apprentices; to anyone who works under a contract personally to do any work for an employer; to contract workers, supplied to do work for an employer by a third party, and to job applicants.
- to trustees and managers of occupational pension schemes (but see Chapter 14 for rules and practices in relation to pension schemes that the Regulations allow).
- to cases where (i) the employment relationship has come to an end (including where the relationship ended before October 2006), (ii) there was an act of age discrimination or harassment during the

relationship, and (iii) the former employee is harassed or discriminated against by being subjected to a detriment, (iv) the former employer is responsible for the harassment or discrimination, and (v) it arises out of and is closely connected to the employment relationship. An example might be if you, the employer, refused to provide a reference for a former employee who could show that they had been subjected to age discrimination (even if it was not unlawful at the time) when they were employed by you.

2. The Regulations outlaw –

- **Direct discrimination.** This is where, on grounds of B's age (or apparent age), you, the employer, treat B less favourably than you treat or would treat others (whose relevant circumstances are the same or not materially different) and you cannot show the treatment is a proportionate means of achieving a legitimate aim.
- **Indirect discrimination.** This is where you, the employer, apply to B a provision, criterion or practice (PCP) which you apply or would apply equally to others not in the same age group as B (whose relevant circumstances are the same or not materially different), but which puts or would put both B and people of his age group at a particular disadvantage when compared with others, and you, the employer, cannot show the PCP is a proportionate means of achieving a legitimate aim.
- **Victimisation.** You, the employer, treat B less favourably than others in the same circumstances, because B has brought a claim under, given evidence in a case under, alleged a contravention of or done anything by reference to the Regulations or because B intends to or you suspect B has done or intends to do any of those things. A false allegation by B not made in good faith is not protected under these provisions.
- **Treating B less favourably than others** in the same circumstances are or would be treated because B has not carried out an instruction to do something discriminatory or because B complains about being given such an instruction. So, for example, disciplining a manager for refusing

to exclude older candidates from consideration for a job would itself be age discrimination.

These are outlawed in the following circumstances –

- in the arrangements you, the employer, make to determine who should be offered a job;
- in the terms on which you offer the job;
- where you refuse to offer, or deliberately do not offer, a job;
- in the terms on which you employ B;
- in the opportunities you, the employer, provide B for promotion, a transfer, training or receiving any other benefit;
- where you refuse to provide B, or deliberately do not provide B, any such opportunity;
- where you dismiss B (including where a fixed-term contract is not renewed or where B is constructively dismissed);
- where you subject B to any other detriment.

3. They also outlaw –

Harassment. This is where, on grounds of age (whether B's or another's), A engages in unwanted conduct which has the purpose or effect of violating B's dignity or creating an environment for B that is intimidating, hostile, degrading, humiliating or offensive. Conduct has the specified effect only if, having regard to all the circumstances, including in particular B's perception, it should reasonably be considered as having that effect. B, for these purposes, is someone who works for A or who has applied to A for employment.

4. They make employers liable –

for any discrimination, harassment or victimisation by their workers in the course of their employment, whether or not it was done with the employer's knowledge or approval

unless they can prove –

they took all the steps that were reasonably practicable to prevent the worker doing the act in question or doing acts of that description in the course of employment.

5. They make unenforceable against the worker –

contract terms whose inclusion amounts to or is in furtherance of, or which provide for, age discrimination against the worker.

6. They make void –

terms of collective agreements or company rules of general application that amount to or are in furtherance of, or which provide for, age discrimination.

7. The Regulations establish –

- a procedure for notifying employees of their intended retirement date and of their right to request not to retire where the employer wishes to enforce retirement;
- a duty to consider requests not to retire and a procedure to be followed for considering such requests.

8. The Regulations allow –

- the dismissal by reason of retirement of an employee aged 65 or over;
- refusal or deliberate omission to offer a job or discrimination in the arrangements made to determine who should be offered a job where B is:
  - over the employer's normal retirement age (NRA) if that is 65 or higher, or
  - if the employer has no NRA, 65, or
  - would reach 65 or an older NRA within six months of his application;

- in relation to the award of any benefit, facility or service (other than one awarded by virtue of B ceasing to work for the employer – such as a 'top-up' redundancy payment), putting B at a disadvantage compared with C, if and to the extent that the disadvantage suffered by B is because B's length of service is less than C's *but*:
  - where B's length of service exceeds five years, it must reasonably appear to the employer that the way it uses the criterion of length of service for awarding the benefit fulfils a business need of its undertaking (for example, by encouraging the loyalty or motivation, or rewarding the experience, of some or all of its workers), and
  - length of service must be either the total length of time the worker has been working for the employer (or any associated employer) or the time he has been doing work which the employer reasonably considers to be at or above a particular level. Periods of absence can be discounted unless it would not be reasonable to do so; so can periods of service prior to a period of absence, if it would be reasonable to do so;
- a wide range of age- or service-related rules and practices in relation to occupational pension schemes, including the fixing of ages for admission to or entitlement under pension schemes and the fixing of different ages for different employees; the use of age criteria in actuarial calculations; differences in pension contributions attributable to pensionable pay; closing schemes to new members or the provision of different schemes for members of different ages or pensionable service;
- paying B less than C is paid where B is paid less than the adult rate of the NMW and the hourly rate of the NMW for someone of B's age is less than that for someone of C's age;
- paying an apprentice not entitled to the NMW less than someone who is entitled to it;
- anything done to comply with a statutory obligation, for example, paying a statutory redundancy payment;

- anything justifiably done to safeguard national security;
- anything done in connection with giving people of a particular age or age group access to training which would help fit them for particular work or encouraging people of a particular age or age group to take advantage of opportunities for doing particular work where it reasonably appears to A that it prevents, or compensates for, disadvantages linked to age suffered by people of that age or age group doing or likely to take up that work (see Chapter 13 on positive action);
- discrimination in recruitment, promotion, transfer, training or dismissal where, having regard to the nature of the employment or the context in which it is carried out, possessing a characteristic related to age is a genuine and determining occupational requirement, it is proportionate to apply that requirement in the particular case and either B does not meet the requirement or A is not satisfied, on reasonable grounds, that B meets it. We think that few characteristics, other than those related to appearance, can genuinely be said to be age-related, so it is unlikely that age-related characteristics are an essential feature of any jobs in manufacturing.

9. The Regulations are enforced –

- by complaint by the worker or job applicant to an employment tribunal
  - within three months of the act complained of;
  - to which the statutory grievance procedure applies (see the EEF publication, *Dispute Resolution: A Practical Guide to the New Law*);
  - in respect of which the complainant may require the employer to complete a statutory questionnaire;
  - in which the complainant has to establish facts from which the tribunal could conclude that the employer has committed or is responsible for an act of discrimination, in which case the tribunal must uphold the complaint unless the employer proves that its

actions or those of its employees were in no sense whatsoever connected with age discrimination or were justified;

- as a result of which the tribunal may award compensation, including for injury to feelings, that is not subject to a statutory maximum.

Appendix 2

Managing an age-inclusive workforce

This section outlines some of the people management aspects of introducing the age discrimination legislation. Learning to treat all workers equally, whatever their age, within every business activity will require for some a learning curve in managerial and employment behaviour and practice. We shall highlight some of the key topics to consider in order to achieve an age-inclusive workplace.

Understanding your workforce

First, in order to develop an age-inclusive culture within your organisation it is essential that your managers understand their workers.

Changes in the workplace

The world of work the younger person enters is very different from the world entered by those over 50. Even for younger employees, working life has changed over the last ten years, but for the older person this change has been radical. Until the 1990s, there was no internet or email; mobile phones, personal computers and faxes were not commonplace and the global market-place was developing alongside technology. Now most people have access to a mobile phone and the internet. Work used to take place in offices, shops and factories mainly between 9 am and 5 pm, Monday to Friday. The pace of life was slower. Today's 24/7 lifestyle with the expectation of immediate response to colleagues and customers is very different.

Pressures on the older worker

The twenty years after the Second World War saw a large increase in the number of children born worldwide. These are commonly known as the 'Baby Boomers' and at present there are 19.8 million of them in the UK. There are specific issues that affect each generation, but the Baby Boomers are a large cohort and are likely to represent at least a quarter of your workforce. This is unprecedented and therefore it is important for managers to be aware of the specific pressures facing this group.

They were the first generation to have their children at a later age due to the introduction of the contraceptive pill, which gave women the freedom to choose how they balanced their lives. Due to an increase of divorce more have had a second family and some a third, which means that many may still have young children, with the emotional and long-term financial demands that this entails. People are living longer so, contrary to expectations, this group may have at least one parent alive in their eighties or nineties. Supporting both the younger and older age group can be difficult and occasionally disruptive to the working day.

This is also the first generation to realise that they are likely to live another 30 years or more, which shapes their decision-making. The prospect of early retirement seemed likely some years ago, but many are now disappointed to find that they will have to work for the foreseeable future due to government policy, commitments and a lack of an adequate pension. They are analysing their health and energy, their finances and the style of work they undertake.

Divorce, remarriage, step-children and single living have all become common lifestyles and have added to the burden of everyday responsibilities and financial pressures.

Managing the pressures faced by your older workers

Managers who understand these pressures and support their employees can work with them and develop new structures and solutions that ensure continued productivity. This is the key to all people management.

Change does not have to be huge, nor does it have to be organisation-wide; small concessions have been shown to enhance morale, health, productivity and retention. To benefit from the contribution that this group of workers can provide, managers need to explore new and flexible ways of working. If managers meet an individual's specific needs, the individual will feel valued and motivated to do a good job.

The majority of the Baby Boomer generation are healthy and energetic and willing to take on new challenges and interests. Managers who find the key to harness this will find themselves with a dynamic, motivated and loyal group of employees and thereby prevent both burnout and resentment, maintaining a stable workforce.

Changing attitudes and stereotypes

Attitudes about age are deeply embedded in people's thinking and behavioural patterns. In order to avoid litigation and promote an age-inclusive culture, managers and employees alike will need to become aware of their own prejudices.

Raising awareness of ageist language

Ageist language such as 'he's having a senior moment', or 'you can't teach an old dog new tricks' are so much part of our culture that we rarely notice them. An 'amusing' birthday card to a 50-year-old work colleague with the legend 'Happy Birthday – now you're over the hill' used to be considered normal practice but is symptomatic of an ageist outlook and could damage working relationships.

You will need to work with your employees to change ingrained ways of responding and to help them to see that many attitudes to age are now outdated. Becoming aware is the first step to change. One of the ways to do this is to keep a note of how often you or others use ageist language in formal and informal settings and raise this as a topic for discussion in your team meetings.

Challenging stereotypes

Stereotypes are shaped by our beliefs, expectations and cultural experiences. Information can often be seen as fact, or reality, instead of an opinion. Challenging outdated beliefs and stereotypes and helping people to understand the consequences of their remarks is an essential step towards change.

Managers need to understand that changing stereotypes needs to be a conscious process and will need constant reinforcement over a period of several months. They will need to ask people to consider why they have used a particular remark, what it actually means and whether it is helpful and relevant. It is important to help them to identify what would have been a more appropriate and constructive statement – for example, 'You must have had a senior moment' could be replaced by 'It looks like you forgot to do X ...'

Training

Management training can help identify alternative ways of thinking, behaving and talking about the issues of age. Organisations need to include age diversity in both their equal opportunities training and management training so as to ensure compliance with the law (see Chapter 13) and integrate best practice.

Managing change

Members of your workforce may assume that an older team member is stuck in the mud. The older person can equally assume that this is how they are regarded and either react by fulfilling this prophecy or feel demotivated by this attitude. But increasing numbers of older people are changing lifestyle at 50-plus and proving that they can manage change and enjoy challenge. There are also plenty of young people who find change difficult.

If change is inevitable, then it is of benefit for people to accept this and make the best of it. It is a choice, but people often forget that they are in control of how they approach a situation. Managers need to help employees see this.

One way to help employees to build confidence in managing continuous change is to identify their innate way of dealing with it through exploring how they have successfully managed change many times in the past in work and home life. Having explored the changes they have undergone during their life, help them to see how they could apply their success strategies in the new situations they face.

It is important for the manager to be aware that different things motivate different people and not to assume that their employees are motivated in the same way as them. People can be motivated by challenge, change, involvement with others, learning, getting results, routine, praise as well as by feeling valued both personally and financially.

Retirement issues and new ways of working

Research studies indicate that:

- 60 per cent of men and 50 per cent of women who retire early do so against their wishes;
- 30 per cent are happy to work until they are 70;
- 13 per cent dread retirement – a feeling that increases with age;
- 80 per cent of Baby Boomers plan to work at least part-time after their official retirement age;
- people are happier at work the older they get.

Whilst there can be benefits to organisations in terms of workforce planning from retaining a retirement age, it gives individuals less flexibility in making their own choice and affects how they view the ten years of their working lives before retirement. In particular, people can see themselves and be seen as 'winding down' to retirement. Some people may feel that a set retirement date renders them past their 'sell by' date, which, obviously, can be demotivating.

If companies decide to do away with a fixed retirement date, individuals, together with their managers, will actively have to decide when it is appropriate for them to retire using different criteria, such as competency, rather than age.

Phased retirement is an alternative. Older people may be seeking different ways of working – for example, three days a week or possibly six months a year. Money is not their only motivator. Self-esteem is often linked to a contribution at work and a sense of purpose in life. The workplace frequently represents an opportunity for fulfilling ambition and gives access to a social life.

It is by no means only older workers and parents who may value the choice to manage their working lives more flexibly. Businesses can frequently benefit from adopting a lateral review of current employment practices to identify new ways to offer employees more flexible employment. Explore with managers and workers opportunities for job-sharing or job-splitting, nine-day fortnights, annualised hours and part-time work. Advances in technology make home working easier. Small changes can make a huge difference to an individual. The ability to create working patterns that reflect the needs of people's lives in the 21st century allows individuals to remain committed and energised to achieve quality of work and life. For example, working from home one day a week, moving to a site nearer home or working flexi-time can revitalise and put a spark back into a demotivated worker.

People frequently just need support at times of real crisis. Where there is an ongoing situation which becomes routine, the individual can manage with less external support from their workplace.

A mutually beneficial way to increase employment opportunities for older workers is to stay in touch with your retirees. This means you can re-employ them to cover maternity leave, sickness and holiday absence. They may also be considered for interim or project work. Temporary help from someone who knows your organisation obviates the need to train a new person.

Leadership and succession planning

HR and line managers are going to need to analyse their organisation's long-term strategy, customer profile and resource requirement in order to provide adequate people resources in the light of the demographic change. As the Baby Boomers retire, organisations risk a mass loss of skills and professional experience. Many areas are already experiencing skills shortages. This means it will be essential to:

- Retain the skills and knowledge required to ensure continued success within your sector.
- Create long-term succession plans.

- Support individuals to contribute fully whilst in the workplace but equally ensure they do not block the promotion of others.

To address talent retention and promotion opportunities for the older worker, the HR department will need to introduce scenario planning to identify possible business needs in 5–10 years' time. Profile your workforce to pinpoint a pool of future talent to provide you with the required competency framework for leadership. This must be an age-neutral process bearing in mind your company's retirement policy.

Developing an age-inclusive organisation will demand good leadership from the top and leaders who walk their talk. There may be entrenched views that some people are too young to do certain jobs or that only older people can be on the board of directors. Managers will need to base decisions on the skills, knowledge and competencies your organisation will need to be successful in future. It may be quite challenging for senior managers to embrace the radical changes to attitude, systems and practice that the age legislation will require.

Performance management and lifelong learning

Performance management is a crucial means to maintaining continued performance and productivity. Some employees may want or be forced to remain at work for financial or social reasons due to changes in retirement age and lifestyle demands such as parenting, caring and pension provision. However, they may not feel sufficiently motivated to contribute fully.

Good performance management is challenging and your managers may need training to ensure that they run appraisals effectively. Appraisals are the ideal way to set objectives that meet both the organisation's and the individual's goals, and achieve win/win results.

Many organisations have had age-related systems for promotion, reward and training, but this will no longer be acceptable unless there is a clear justification. Appraisal forms and procedures will need to be reviewed to ensure that they are age-inclusive and based on competencies.

Many assumptions about workers' productivity and their ability to learn as they get older are unfounded, but people complain that their managers can 'give up on them' or, in the case of younger workers, think they are not experienced enough to take on a new role. Some are shunted sideways, some left to get bored. It is important to see that people have potential to learn and grow at any stage of life. Companies should not use age as a criterion for deciding who should be promoted, who should set up a new department or who should drive a new project. Competencies are the way forward.

Managers will also need to find the key to motivating a demotivated older worker in 'waiting for retirement' mode. Career progression is not just promotion. Many will have progressed to where they feel comfortable. This does not mean they want to feel bored. Exploring lateral uses for a person's skills, or retraining them, can be rejuvenating for someone who for many years carried out the same role.

One of the ways to inspire both older and younger workers is to set up a mentoring programme. This enables your organisation to profit from the experience and expertise of older employees who can share their knowledge with others. This recognition of their value to the organisation is motivating and research shows that all parties benefit.

Lifelong learning

As a general rule, company training must now be open to all age groups. Bear in mind that many older people have fewer qualifications than their direct reports and may feel anxious about learning in front of younger, better qualified employees. Be sensitive to these situations and, through the appraisal process, help older people identify their preferred learning method and encourage them to continue to develop their potential. They in turn bring a sense of perspective and training courses could provide a helpful opportunity for knowledge sharing.

Intergenerational teamworking

Until recently the hierarchy within many organisations was specifically related to age. This has been turned on its head and younger people are increasingly likely to be found in senior positions. An older person could have a boss who is both years younger than them and better qualified. This can be challenging to both parties.

Some younger managers report that they can find it difficult to manage older people, who may be the same age as their parents or even a grandparent. 'I am younger than them, they have been doing this work for ages – how can I delegate in this situation!'

In order to manage this situation, encourage employees to put age aside and to approach work situations 'in role' rather than in a personal and subjective way. It is important that they feel confident of their skills and competencies rather than perceiving themselves as members of a particular generation. The same approach can be used to help the older worker deal with issues of ego and to accept that someone younger than them has reached a higher position and has a lot to offer.

An intergenerational group can enhance creativity and contribute a powerful mix of new ideas with wisdom, experience and perspective. It is not just young people who have new ideas, nor older people who have perspective. Mixed-age teams can break down these misconceptions and stereotypes so as to enhance creativity and innovation. All your workers, young and old, should be encouraged to be open to new ideas and to articulate their experiences in a way that is positive and relevant. Everyone, including those who are new to the workplace, should be encouraged to feel confident to express their ideas.

With thanks to contributors Keren Smedley and Helen Whitten at Age Talks (www.agetalks.com).

Appendix 3

Health, work and well-being

Myths surrounding an ageing workforce

Various 'myths' surround the health and abilities of the older worker. The Health and Safety Laboratory (HSL), which is linked to the Health and Safety Executive, undertook some research in 2005 into these myths:

1. Chronological age determines health, and age brings illness and disease.
2. Getting old is associated with loss of cognitive capacity (mental processes such as memory, problem-solving and understanding).
3. Older workers have less physical strength and endurance.
4. Older workers tend to have poorer sensory abilities, such as sight and hearing.
5. Older adults have difficulty adapting to change.
6. Older adults find it harder to learn new information, making their knowledge and skills outdated.
7. Older workers take more time off work.
8. Older workers have more accidents in the workplace.
9. Older workers are less productive.

The report found evidence to support only two of these; the remainder are, indeed, myths, and not based in fact. There was some basis for the belief that cognitive capacity and sensory abilities decline with age, but even here the evidence is specific to individuals and cannot be generalised to all older workers. And in the specific cases where they do apply, the report indicates that small adaptations in work equipment (for example, using larger computer text size for those with deteriorating eyesight) can often compensate. It follows that employers have little basis, in terms of the health and abilities of older workers, for declining to recruit and retain such workers and, consequently, that they may find it difficult to justify to a tribunal discrimination against older workers that is not expressly permitted by the Regulations.

Workforce health profile

Ill-health can affect workers of all ages. In a pool of 100 workers, one might expect evidence of at least 100 health disorders. Not that every employee will be ill; some employees may have more than one condition. The impact on the organisation of this typical worker ill-health profile is that at any one time some of the employees will be absent from work, some will be at work but not performing adequately and others will be at work with no noticeable performance issues although some in fact have an illness.

As the HSL report notes, 'the risk of poor health does increase with age; however, ageing is a very individual process. Many of the causes of illness can be prevented or minimised through, for example, fitness training, stopping smoking, weight control, etc. Chronological age is therefore not the most important or accurate determinant of health; aspects such as lifestyle play a more important role in determining individuals' well being'. None the less, it is likely that the rate for a number of ill-health conditions (cancers, diabetes, heart disease, hernias, arthritis) increases with an older workforce. For example, of workers aged 50–59, around 15–22 per cent of professional/managerial workers and 33 per cent of manual workers have a long-term limiting health condition. The vast majority of these health conditions are not going to be caused by work, but some may be exacerbated by it.

Impacts of worker ill-health

Ill-health is both an important cause of people leaving work before state pension age (SPA) and a barrier to returning to work. Currently, there are 2.6 million individuals aged between 50 and SPA who are out of work. Recent research has shown that ill-health was the most common reason people gave for leaving their most recent job, and was mentioned by 46 per cent of those under SPA and not in work.

Health status is the most important single factor pushing people out of work and reducing the likelihood that they will return. The earlier the retirement the more it is driven by health as opposed to financial factors. Men and women in lower social class groups are more likely to cite health-related reasons for leaving work ahead of SPA; those in physical or heavy manual jobs are especially likely to have low expectations of working up to or beyond SPA. The likelihood of someone who leaves work through ill-health or disability after age 50 re-entering the labour market is slim, and declines rapidly as the length of unemployment increases.

Research shows that people working with health conditions often had a strong work ethic and a desire for independence from state benefits. Employer support, such as flexible working arrangements, was cited as important in helping those with health conditions to remain in or return to work.

A DWP research report found that people working after SPA felt there were health benefits to remaining in work and keeping active. Paid work was seen as something which could make a positive contribution to physical and psychological health. In particular men who were often considerably older than SPA attributed their good health partly to being able to continue in valued jobs which kept their minds and bodies active. The research also indicates that people do not generally seek to stay in work or at the same levels of work when no longer capable – a concern which some employers have raised.

Factors such as these are encouraging employers to go beyond mere compliance with current legislation and to aim to achieve real cultural change.

Influencing the health and well-being of the ageing workforce

There are a number of actions an employer can take to make the workplace more age-friendly. Many of these are not age-specific and will benefit all workers, thus increasing the prospects for a healthy older workforce in the future.

1. Consider changing the patterns of work (e.g. change from a three-shift system to a day or double-day system).
2. Consider changing employees' tasks or work content (e.g. remove or alter part of the job, taking into account that the experienced older worker may know a more efficient approach to the task).
3. Consider adaptations to the workplace (e.g. altering the layout of the work area).
4. Consider adaptations to the pace of work.
5. Consider adaptations to tools and equipment (good ergonomic design – e.g. large-diameter handles for workers with arthritis – is equally beneficial to younger workers).
6. Provide for mobility (e.g. a car parking space for those who have difficulty walking).
7. Undertake a risk assessment and implement an action plan for minimising:
    - work-related stress,
    - musculoskeletal disorders,
    - exposure to tobacco smoke.
8. Establish a policy for dealing with alcohol and other substance abuse.
9. Encourage physical activity, such as walking or cycling to work and using the stairs rather than the lifts.
10. Encourage healthy eating and, if catering is provided, ensure healthy options are available.

Appendix 4

Sample retirement policy (for retirement age of 65)

Note: Be aware of your obligations under the disability discrimination legislation when considering issues relating to ill-health.

A. Scope of the policy

This policy applies to the retirement of [all employees] [employees in specified grade or department]. It does not confer any contractual entitlement, and the Company ('we') may at any time at our discretion make changes to the policy or remove it altogether.

B. Retirement age

The retirement age of [all employees] [employees in specified grade or department] is 65. You have the statutory right to request not to retire.

It is our Company policy that [all employees] [employees in specified grade or department] should retire when they reach the retirement age of 65.

However, you have the statutory right to request not to retire. If you make a request in accordance with the relevant legal requirements (see below), then we will give it careful consideration. We may agree to you continuing to work beyond the retirement age if we think that exceptional circumstances apply.

C. Procedure prior to retirement

At least six months before you reach the retirement age, [HR Manager] will write to you to confirm that this date is your intended date of retirement and to inform you that you have the statutory right to request not to retire.

If you wish to exercise your statutory right to request, you must do so in writing no later than three months before the intended date of retirement. You should send your request to [HR Manager].

You must send your request within this time scale. If you send a request late, and/or if it does not meet the requirements set out below, then we are not obliged by law to consider it.

By law, your request must:

- be in writing;
- state that it is made under paragraph 5(3) of Schedule 6 of the Employment Equality (Age) Regulations 2006; and
- propose that your employment should continue indefinitely, or for a specified period, or until a specified date.

In addition (although this is not required by law) we encourage you to identify in your request any issues you think we should take into account in considering it and in particular explain why you think that exceptional circumstances apply in your case (see Section D below for examples). Including such information in your request will assist us to consider it.

On receipt of a request that meets these requirements, we will invite you to a meeting to discuss it (unless we agree to your request, in which case we will notify you of this). The meeting will normally be held by your line manager. Both parties must take all reasonable steps to attend the meeting.

Following the meeting we will give you our decision in writing. We are not required by law to give reasons for our decision.

If our decision is to refuse your request, or to allow your employment to continue for a shorter period than that which you proposed, then you have the right to appeal. If you wish to appeal, you must send an appeal letter setting out the grounds of your appeal. We will then invite you to an appeal meeting. Following the appeal meeting we will give you our decision in writing.

You have the right to be accompanied by a fellow worker at the meeting and appeal meeting.

D. Considering a request not to retire

We will give careful consideration to any request made which meets the requirements set out above.

In assessing your request, we will consider whether any exceptional circumstances apply to you. In general, we will not agree to a request if, in our view, no exceptional circumstances apply.

Examples of exceptional circumstances are:

- you are a key worker with no current replacement;
- there is a serious shortage of employees with your skills;
- your continued employment would enable you to pass on your skills and/or to train others;
- your continued employment would enable you to assist in the completion of a specific task or project.

In considering your request, we may seek the views of your line manager and other employees. We may also consult your performance appraisals and your attendance and disciplinary records.

Appendix 5

Sample standard notification

Note: if you use this wording for a fall-back notification, you cannot impose a time limit for the employee to make a request.

[*Date*]

Dear [*employee*]

I am writing to inform you that the intended date of your retirement is [*date*].

You have the statutory right to make a request not to retire on this date. If you wish to make a request, you must do so no later than [*date that is three months before the intended date of retirement*]. The request should be marked for my attention.

If you do not make a request by this date, then you will lose your statutory right to have your request considered and your retirement will take effect on [*intended date of retirement*].

I enclose a copy of the Company's retirement policy, which explains the procedure that applies if you make a request in time. The policy also explains what must be contained in your request.

Yours sincerely,

Appendix 6

Sample letters required under procedure for considering requests

Inviting employee to meeting

[*Date*]

Dear [*employee*]

I am writing to inform you that a meeting will be held to discuss your request not to retire. The meeting will be held on [*insert date*] at [*insert time*] at [*insert location*].

You have the right to be accompanied at the meeting by a fellow worker (this includes a trade union representative, providing that they work for the Company). Your companion can address the meeting but cannot answer questions on your behalf, although you can confer with your companion during the meeting.

After the meeting we will inform you in writing of the Company's decision. If our decision is to accept your request, then we will confirm that we agree to you working beyond retirement either indefinitely or for a specified period. If our decision is to reject your request, then we will confirm that your intended date of retirement is [*insert date*]. You will have the right to appeal if our decision is to reject your request or to allow you to continue working for a shorter period than you requested.

Yours sincerely,

Refusal of request

Note: this sample is intended to complement the sample retirement policy in Appendix 4

[*Date*]

Dear [*employee*]

Following our meeting on [*date*] to discuss your request not to retire, I am writing to inform you of the Company's decision.

Unfortunately, we have decided to refuse your request because, in accordance with the Company's retirement policy, no exceptional circumstances apply. I therefore confirm that we still wish you to retire. Retirement will take place on [*insert intended date of retirement – this should be the date given in the standard notification*]. Your employment will terminate on this date.

You have the right to appeal this decision. If you wish to do so, please inform […] in writing, setting out the grounds of your appeal. You should do so as soon as reasonably practicable.

Yours sincerely,

Acceptance of request – no fixed period

[*Date*]

Dear [*employee*]

Following our meeting on [*date*] to discuss your request not to retire, I am writing to inform you of the Company's decision.

The Company has decided to accept your request. We have decided that your employment should continue indefinitely.

Yours sincerely,

Acceptance of request – fixed period

[*Date*]

Dear [*employee*]

Following our meeting on [*date*] to discuss your request not to retire, I am writing to inform you of the Company's decision.

The Company has decided to accept your request. We have decided that your employment should continue for a specified period. Your employment will continue for a period of [*insert length*]. At the expiry of this period, we intend you to retire.

You have the right to appeal this decision. If you wish to do so, please inform [*HR Manager*] in writing, setting out the grounds of your appeal. You should do so as soon as reasonably practicable.

Yours sincerely,

After appeal: refusal of request

[*Date*]

Dear [*employee*]

We held a meeting on [*date*] to discuss your appeal against the Company's decision concerning your request not to retire. I am writing to inform you of the Company's decision.

The Company has decided to refuse your request and I confirm that we still wish you to retire. Retirement will take place on [*insert intended date of retirement – this should be the date given in the standard notification*]. Your employment will terminate on this date.

Yours sincerely,

After appeal: acceptance of request – no fixed period

[*Date*]

Dear [*employee*]

We held a meeting on [*date*] to discuss your appeal against the Company's decision concerning your request not to retire. I am writing to inform you of the Company's decision.

The Company has decided to accept your request. We have decided that your employment should continue indefinitely.

Yours sincerely,

After appeal: acceptance of request – fixed period

[*Date*]

Dear [*employee*]

We held a meeting on [*date*] to discuss your appeal against the Company's decision concerning your request not to retire. I am writing to inform you of the Company's decision.

The Company has decided to accept your request. We have decided that your employment should continue for a specified period. Your employment will continue for a period of [*insert length*]. At the expiry of this period, we intend you to retire.

Yours sincerely,

Index